PREFACE

As the inaugural publication of the International Art Museum of America, *International Art Museum of America – A Portion of Its Artwork* has naturally become a very collectable book. This book gathers the arts of calligraphy, painting, sculpture and architecture into a single corpus, and was published in order to provide all visitors of the Museum a memento after they have viewed the exhibition, as well as to provide art lovers a reference for learning by example. The book also aims to attract more people to visit this classically elegant yet resplendent museum, which possesses a distinctive artistic style that differs from that of all other art museums in the world.

In designing this book, we decided to incorporate not only some artistic scenes from inside the museum building but also a subset of the artwork currently displayed. We have also included enlarged details of portions of particular pieces in order to provide appreciators and students of art an opportunity for nuanced observation and close examination. We would especially like to mention that the pieces exhibited at the Museum belong to the highest order of world-class art. The likes of certain pieces exhibited at the Museum cannot be found in any other museum in the entire world!

Since these precious works of art are unquestionably unique in this world, as agreed by experts, we decided to issue this souvenir book to promote the circulation and thereby appreciation of the Museum's art, in hopes of adding luster to human culture and art, and serving the people of the United States and of the world.

International Art Museum of America

TABLE OF CONTENTS

TABLE OF CONTENTS

TABLE OF CONTENTS

TABLE OF CONTENTS

TABLE OF CONTENTS

TABLE OF CONTENTS

INTRODUCTION

Located at the heart of downtown San Francisco, on 1025 Market Street near Sixth Street, the International Art Museum of America is a permanent, non-profit museum open to the public. The Museum's goal is to utilize the exhibition forum to pass on works of art that have achieved the most exquisite beauty and preciousness in the history of civilization, in order to further humanity's moral progress, spiritual wellbeing, cultural development and world peace. It takes as its mission bringing humanity happiness and uplifting aesthetic enjoyment.

By resolution of its board of directors, the International Art Museum of America was originally designated to permanently display the artwork of H.H. Dorje Chang Buddha III, the only artist to receive the World Peace Prize. However, His Holiness the Buddha adamantly disagreed, expressing His opinion that the International Art Museum of America is a site for the masters of art worldwide to showcase their artistic accomplishments, and should embrace diversity in order to provide the public with broader aesthetic enjoyment. The Board of Directors yielded to this suggestion of His Holiness the Buddha.

As an international public art museum, the International Art Museum of America is committed to assuring that the exhibited artworks meet discerning world-class standards of excellence. Thus, all artworks held or displayed by the International Art Museum of America have been approved by a majority vote of the Museum's Board of Directors. The Board of Directors have established their criteria for artwork selection as follows:

"Regardless of the medium – whether it be painting or calligraphy, ink-wash painting, oil painting, watercolor, gouache, or sculpture – the artwork must come from the hands of a world-class or national artist, and the value of artworks by any such living artist must be within the highest, or second-highest tier of valuation. Any artist whose work has not been valued above two hundred thousand dollars per square foot must have been exhibited by the highest governmental body of his or her nation, or be an eminent artist and the director of an art museum or head of an art academy, in order for the artists' work to be considered. Finally, the work of any artist to be exhibited must be valued at a minimum of two hundred thousand dollars per square foot. Additionally, artists who lived over one hundred years ago are exempt from the valuation minimums, but must be exhibited at two or more art museums of worldwide renown, and have produced artwork of exceptional quality, to be considered for exhibition at the International Art Museum of America. The Museum is concerned only with the quality of the artwork itself, not with the number of artists who are selected for exhibition."

These are the basic criteria by which the International Art Museum of America considers artworks for exhibition. Thus the artworks that are able to be selected for exhibition by the International Art Museum of America are mostly unparalleled artworks, exquisite works of rarified realms, or the paragons of their respective schools or types of art. For example, the Museum exhibits representative works from each subject-category and period of H.H. Dorje Chang Buddha III, the selling price of whose paintings figure among the highest of living artists. Among the highest valued of such paintings were appraised at over thirty-five million dollars and over fifty million dollars, respectively, and are still continuing to appreciate. To take another example, the U.S. Congressional Record has hailed the lotus paintings of artist Yu Hua Shouzhi Wang as "unsurpassed" in "the history of Chinese art," and her painted sculptures of cobblestones and sculptures of coral formations as "treasures of the world."

These are all highly valued gems of art. The Museum possesses not only calligraphy and oil painting but also the most accomplished artworks in the history of Chinese paintings, which surpass the traditional masters in subject-categories such as Flora, Fauna, Birds and Insects, landscape, and portraiture. Some realistic works not only appear exactly like their object but are more exquisitely detailed and beautiful than their real-life counterpart. The International Art Museum of America also boasts exquisite frame art – such as those that are sculpted then finished by oil painting, formed in the style of branches or of jade slabs entwined with withered vines – not found anywhere else in the world. Moreover, the Museum houses a piece proclaimed as the "peerless treasure of the world" and whose value is incalculable: the first artwork in human history in which the sculpture of a stone enfolds mist that never dissipates.

In addition, the Museum will present, in several groups and stages, exhibitions of irreplicable artwork – seen for the first time in thousands of years – whose ethereal beauty captivates the soul. Examples include "Wondrous

Resplendency," "Tacit Understanding Expressed Through a Soft Smile," "Beauty Draped Over Rock," "Yellow Yellow," "A Holy Song at the Dharma Assembly of the Sakyamuni Buddha," "Song of a Majestic Boulder," "Mysterious Boulder with Mist," "Forever Brilliant," and "A Pillar Holds Up Heaven." These Yun sculptures are treasures of art whose consummate beauty justifies their title as the acme of world-class art.

Also, the Museum will present rotating exhibitions of sculptures of corals and vases that are created from wood and stone and then painted to convey the essence of natural coral but surpass its beauty, the likes of which are truly found nowhere else. These works include "A Pastel Adornment," "Sea God," "White Jade Treasure," "Supreme Treasure of the Dragon King's Palace – King," "Supreme Treasure of the Dragon King's Palace – Phoenix Treasure," "Sea Palace Monarch," "Wondrous Coral of the Sea Valley," "Blush Red," "Parched Ancient Coral" and more, all of which are paired with unique artistic vases. Other rare treasures of the art world include " Sheep Tallow Jade," "Ceramic of the Victorious Monarch," "Lustrous Oils Vase," "Embroidered Red Dress," "Art as Tender and Pure as a Baby," "Tall Emerald Vase," "Mottled Enamel Porcelain," and "A Vibrantly Colored Ceramic Glimpsed." Art critics have commented that since these Yun sculptures and wondrous coral artworks appeared on this earth, even the most extravagant jewels and jades lost their luster, just as the stars pale against a resplendent moon. The comparison makes it easy to imagine how stirring, intoxicating and exhilarating an aesthetic enjoyment the artwork exhibited by the International Art Museum of America provides.

In conclusion, therefore, the art exhibited at the International Art Museum of America is undoubtably unique in this world. The Museum is headed by renowned figures: the Honorary President of International Art Museum of America was the late Marquis Juan Antonio Samaranch, who was the lifetime Honorary Chairman of the International Olympic Committee, and the Museum's Honorary Art Director is Ching-Kuo Wu, Ph.D., who is President of the International Boxing Association.

A Glimpse into

International Art Museum of America

H.H. Dorje Chang Buddha III

This bust is a realistic portrait by Professor Wang Zhibin, a member of China's International Artists Association and International Sculptors Association. Wang's work has been exhibited at many municipal and provincial exhibitions and has won numerous awards.

Dorje Chang Buddha is, in Buddhism, the first and most ancient sambhogakaya Buddha in the universe. All of the other Buddhas, such as Amitabha Buddha, attained Buddhahood through learning and practicing Buddha-dharma transmitted by Dorje Chang Buddha. H.H. Dorje Chang Buddha III is the third true incarnation of Dorje Chang Buddha. This identity is not self-conferred but confirmed, in strict adherence to the regulations of the recognition system of Tibetan Buddhism, by leaders of Buddhist sects worldwide.

In this world, H.H. Dorje Chang Buddha III has not only been recognized as achieving the highest status, but has received more recognition certifications and demonstrated more accomplishments than anyone else in the past few thousand years: the book *H.H. Dorje Chang Buddha III* alone displays accomplishments in thirty large categories. This museum, similarly, exhibits only a portion of H.H. Dorje Chang Buddha III's artistic attainments, which in turn constitutes only a portion of His countless accomplishments. The artworks of His Holiness the Buddha are very valuable in the world. Finally, the magnanimity and immaculate moral character of H.H. Dorje Chang Buddha III, His exceeding compassion in benefiting others, and His outstanding contributions to humanity have all been recognized by innumerable world-class awards.

(#37)

Xiang Tu Huai Qing (Nostalgia for the Homeland) (#37)

Artist: H.H. Dorje Chang Buddha III
Style: Xiangtong

Reaching the highest realm in Chinese calligraphy and painting requires inheriting tradition while pioneering new styles. Innovation in Chinese painting and calligraphy must be grounded in tradition, or else it becomes mere scribble that is neither Western nor Chinese. While a few blind scribblings lacking any spirit or import have become famous or popular, the judgment of the uninformed ultimately never qualifies such works to stand as treasures of the ink and brush.

The strokes of truly successful Chinese painting and calligraphy must rise above the mundane yet escape artifice, and exude a scholarly air and the aura of ancient stone seals. Artists who aspire to a level of artistic creation that exceeds even masterpiece status must reign in his mature painting style for a subdued hand, shedding all superficial flourishes. Described as a mature hand within a childlike state, such a hand returns to the source. The painting includes everything from innocent whimsy to jagged strokes resembling inscriptions on ancient stone seals. Mature brushwork is nevertheless applied with a childlike mindset, with a painterly hand that moves freely, unselfconsciously, and without inhibition. Spontaneous brushstrokes appear at once painterly and calligraphic, apparent clumsiness veils controlled elegance, power is deftly internalized, and spirit is not drawn but expressed – only then does an artwork achieve ultimate class and truly embody spirit.

The brushwork and spirit of "Nostalgia for the Homeland" reaches just such a level. This artwork is painted in the "Xiangtong" style. A photograph of a reproduction of this painting was featured in previous publications, and bore the simple inscription of "Yee." The original painting was only recently inscribed with "Dorje Chang III," and stamped with a three-dimensional, eight-jewel, gold-inlaid fingerprint seal.

The full inscription reads: "Twenty-six springs have passed, and feelings for the homeland pervade the scroll. Years past saw duplicate copies, and today this inscription completes the original. Twenty-six years have been borne away by impermanence, and this original painting has long been preserved secretly. The images in the books show reproductions of the original work. As the former inscription was lacking, the genuine piece I left for this day to inscribe. For the same reason, over thirty exquisite pieces, including 'Year of the Buffalo,' 'After the Rain,' 'Mist, Clouds, and Autumnal Color,' 'Lotus Flowers and Fish,' and 'Brushwork that Has Reached a Holy State' also receive their authenticating inscriptions today. All pieces stamped with the three-dimensional, eight-jewel, gold-inlaid fingerprint seal are genuine. – Dorje Chang III"

Temple of Good Fortune and Wisdom (#36)

Artist: H.H. Dorje Chang Buddha III

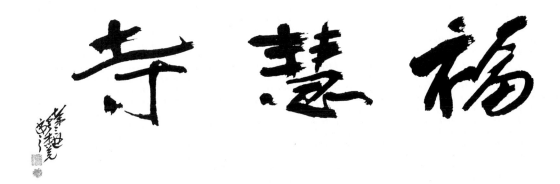

The characteristic feature of this calligraphic work is firmness seen within gentleness. Although casually written with natural strokes of the brush, one can see a vigorous and powerful quality born of strong calligraphic skills on the highest level. If one does not have a solid foundation in stone inscriptions, one could not possibly attain such a marvelous mastery of calligraphy. "Temple of Good Fortune and Wisdom" is an inscription written for a Buddhist temple.

Two Lotus Flowers, One Lotus Capsule, One Dharma Nature (#55) (partial picture)

Artist: H.H. Dorje Chang Buddha III

"Two Lotus Flowers, One Lotus Capsule, One Dharma Nature" was created after H.H. Dorje Chang Buddha III came to the United States. The technique of freehand brushwork in simple strokes was used, as was the technique of supplementing the scene with fascinating charm. Various elegant brushwork styles were blended into one whole to create an image of harmonious beauty. The inherent essence of the lotus flowers was brought forth with a very small number of brush strokes. Only a few strokes were used to paint each flower, yet they look so real, beautiful, alive, elegant, and enchanting. These vibrant flowers reflect the artist's experienced hand that created them. They even convey a three-dimensional, fresh feeling. Although this work of art appears very simple, it in fact is far from ordinary. From the stems of the lotus flowers, one can immediately discern the flavor of stone seal engravings. Therefore, no additional touches are needed on the stems. The key fact is that, with just one stroke of the brush for each stem, quality of the highest order is naturally expressed. This is a state of artistry that is extremely difficult to achieve. In addition to such interesting brushwork are the design and colors of the flower vase. Charming clusters produce the effect of a natural marble pattern. It looks completely real without any trace of artificiality.

The meaning of the title "Two Lotus Flowers, One Lotus Capsule, One Dharma Nature" is that these two lotus flowers and one lotus capsule give expression to the original nature of everything in the universe. That is, the source of the highest state of artistry is the wisdom that springs forth from one's original nature. Such art belongs to the Craftsmanship Vidya, which is one of the Five Vidyas.

Qing Cheng (#177) (Mount Qingcheng)

Artist: H.H. Dorje Chang Buddha III
Style: Wenfeng

"Mount Qingcheng" is an ink-and-wash painting done in the "Wenfeng" style. This work was created using the center brush-tip technique applied in calligraphy. Inspired by a free and natural artistic conception, the artist's brush strokes and coloring were not applied deliberately. Instead, the entire painting was created in one continuous stream of inspiration.

The painting depicts a scenic view located on Mount Qingcheng in Sichuan, China. In studying the application of brush strokes and ink, we can see how extremely mature the artist's skills are. Those skills enabled the artist to create this painting imbued with such a scholarly air.

La Jolie Fille de Arles
(#340)

Artist: Henri Joseph Duwee (1810~1884)

Entitled in French "La Jolie Fille de Arles" or "The Pretty Girl from Arles," this large and important work by Duwee dates to around 1880. It is typical of the quality of painting Duwee produced during his long and illustrious career.

Born in Brussels in 1810, the son of the celebrated painter Henri Duwee, the young man soon showed a precocious talent as an artist. He took his first lessons from his father, but while still in his early teens he became a student of the most famous figure painter in the Lowlands at the time, Francois-Joseph Navez. It was Navez that convinced the young artist to pursue a career as a figure painter with a particular emphasis on historical works.

From 1833 he exhibited his artwork widely, including exhibitions in Ghent and Brussels. Soon his reputation spread to other countries, and he was invited to show his paintings at important venues in Berlin and Vienna. His paintings were always of the highest standards, with a realistic attention to detail and a sentimentality of subject. In this particular example, we see a pretty young girl dressed in the fashion of the day standing by a wall. Duwee's works are collected by many museums, such as the Museum of Amsterdam in the Netherlands and the Museum of Saint-Gilles in Belgium.

Gao Ge Zhi Yun
(High Quality Charm)
(#2)

Artist: H.H. Dorje Chang Buddha III

This painting may appear very simple at first glance, yet why does it reveal a feeling of comfort and ease? It indeed evidences a high state of artistic mastery found in Chinese paintings, a state in which the artist returns from familiarity to spontaneity. This state of realization enables people to feel the spirit behind the brush strokes, colors, and charming appearance. Painted with a relaxed hand and free mind, it displays both the adeptness of an experienced elderly painter and the innocence of youth. Its brush strokes reflect a mind free of attachment and a scene of red plum blossoms that may appear somewhat chaotic but actually is not.

Still-Life with a Vase of Peonies (#352)

Artist: Hubert Bellis (1831~1902)

Although not a true Impressionist, the later paintings of Hubert Bellis clearly show the influence that the French Impressionists had on his work.

Born in Brussels in 1831, Bellis was a pupil at the Brussels Academy, where he received instruction from the great Belgian portrait painter, Navez. Continuing his education at the atelier of Henri de Coene, he decided from a young age to devote his career to still-life painting. His paintings of fruit, flowers and frequently shellfish were extremely well received by the public and critics alike and garnered Bellis a tremendous reputation. This superb example of his work shows him at his very best. Dating to around 1900, Bellis clearly illustrates why he is now regarded as one of Belgium's most distinguished and collectable "nature-morte" painters.

After a long and distinguished career, Hubert Bellis died at St. Joost-ten-Noode in 1902. Paintings by the artist are collected by the Municipal Museum of Amsterdam, the Victoria State Art Gallery in Melbourne, Australia and many other museums.

Du Shi Hong Tou Wan Li Gui (#209) (Red-Headed Eagle on a Lone Rock After Having Returned From Thousands of Miles Away)

Artist: H.H. Dorje Chang Buddha III

Actually, not much need be said about this painting. It presents itself as being plain and simple, for un-elaborate brushwork was used to create it. Nonetheless, a spirited look is manifested through the painting skills of the artist, which are based on his wondrous state of mind. Every touch of the brush expresses the artist's masterly inner-skills. Each stroke is backed by solid knowledge and experience. There is a special interplay of color and charm. The style of this painting, which is abstract, was created solely by H.H. Dorje Chang Buddha III.

Su Shi Nao Chun (partial picture)
(Twittering Sparrows in Early Spring) (#18)

Artist: H.H. Dorje Chang Buddha III   Style: Fanpu

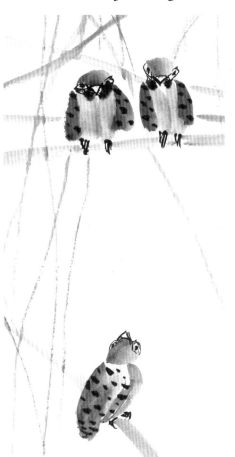

Wielding the brush freely and effortlessly, the artist used only a small number of brush strokes to depict this relaxed and delightful motif. Spring is in the air, the sun shines gently, the breezes are pleasant, and branches are sprouting leaves. A group of sparrows perched on branches are enjoying themselves to their hearts' content. As a poem states, "On a sunny day with light wind, nobody has any cares. This enrapturing scene of nature is for all to enjoy, yet only birds are having fun playing about." These birds look calm and at ease as they chirp softly and call out loudly. They seem to be heartily singing a light melody. All of this makes for a lovely and peaceful scene that is full of life, leisurely, highly elegant, and deeply absorbing. This artwork is in the "Fanpu" style.

Mo Zong (#10)
(Palm Tree in Ink)

Artist: H.H. Dorje Chang Buddha III

"Palm Tree in Ink" painted by H.H. Dorje Chang Buddha III contains a type of unearthly charm. As Master Liu Kaiqu, Director of the National Art Gallery of China, stated, "This painting displays the refined techniques of the ancients as well as new ideas. Its excellence springs from its simple and pure design, the profound dexterity of the artist, and the natural, rich charm of the image that is pleasing to the eye and comforting to the mind."

Shan Jian Yuan Xue
(Going to a Faraway School in the Mountains) (#39)

Artist: H.H. Dorje Chang Buddha III
Style: Banqi

This painting is in the "Banqi "style. It portrays children who live in a mountain area going to school. Children who live in mountain areas go to school on foot. Day after day, they cross over mountains and ravines on their way to and from school where they study diligently. They face many more difficulties than do city children. Therefore, they should all the more treasure their opportunities and exert themselves in the pursuit of knowledge so that they can become talented persons who benefit others!

The technique applied in this painting is very unusual. Artistic appeal can be seen everywhere in this brushwork. Even tiny touches of the brush contain a charm born of dense and light hues of ink and color. However, out of vigorous, bold, and seasoned brushwork, the effect of a picture made from an engraved plate is produced. Every brush stroke displays the traditional style of stone seals. An interesting look is also revealed where brush strokes sometimes break and continue.

Gao Zu Bao Ma Xi (High-Leg Treasure Horses) (#225)

Artist: H.H. Dorje Chang Buddha III   Style: Menglong

The High-Leg Treasure Horse is a thoroughbred horse with great stamina. When this treasure horse perspires, it appears to be bleeding due to the color of its perspiration. According to ancient legend, it is the most precious among all species of horses. It has the reputation of being able to travel over three hundred miles a day. Long mane hairs and a mighty, strong-willed, handsome appearance are its prominent characteristics.

The High-Leg Treasure Horses in this painting have longer legs than horses commonly seen in paintings. The hairs of their manes are also long and strong. An extremely rare brushwork technique that combines haziness with clarity was applied to paint the hairs of the horses. The gossamer-thin hairs are strong

(partial picture)

but pliable. One can clearly see the natural effect of sunlight on the horses' manes. Moreover, contrasting variations of dark and light are seen in every hair. The hairs of the horses are depicted with a realistic effect that nonetheless transcend their natural look.

An artistic technique was used to thoroughly capture on paper the charm and atmosphere of the grassland, lake, sky, and land. The "haziness technique" was applied to express a state of realization in which there is no distinction between emptiness and form.

The ancient cypress tree was drawn in one shade of green without the need to add decorative touches in several different shades of green. Both the spirit and form of the tree were captured through the artist's brush. In addition, elegant charm is revealed by a small number of dots of red leaves in the background that compliment the scene. The most difficult part of this work of art was painting the roots, trunk, and leaves in a spontaneous, casual manner using the center brush-tip technique yet maintaining a scholarly tone. Such mastery of painting cannot be easily attained and requires solid skills in calligraphy, literature, and painting as well as a noble moral character.

From the brushwork style and details of this painting, we can sense the profound inner-cultivation of a renowned scholar. The abilities of a literary giant with abundant talent are visible everywhere. The scholarly tone and brushwork style are skillful and vigorous, totally free of any trace of the mundane, and reflect the highest level of painting and calligraphy. Anyone who lifts a brush in an attempt to paint such painting will appreciate the fact that this scholarly style cannot be accomplished by anyone other than a literary giant who is a great master of art.

This painting coherently unites realism and small-scale freehand brushwork as well as the use of haze and clarity.

Fragrant Loofah in a Purple-Bamboo Forest (#277)

Artist: H.H. Dorje Chang Buddha III
Style: Weiyin

On the darkest of nights, the sudden inspiration for this painting flashed into the artist's consciousness, giving birth to the artistic charm and allure embodied in this work. The rhythm of color galloped across the canvas as soon as the flying brush strokes were completed.

Moonlight reveals green loofah on branches in the endlessly intriguing purple-bamboo forest. The loofah and purple-bamboo form a delightful contrast. The vastness of the night conveys the work's artistic sentiments.

This painting appears to be simple. Its brushwork, however, reflects extraordinary experience and maturity, evoking the paintings of sunflowers by Van Gogh. Although the colors are simple, they reveal a boundless artistic spirit. How could the elegance of such fragrant loofah in a purple-bamboo forest not live on forever?

Everlasting Wondrous Appeal (#279)

Artist: H.H. Dorje Chang Buddha III
Style: Weiyin

On its surface, this is an impressionist painting. Large clusters of colors manifest subtle changes. Standing near the painting, one sees clusters of colors painted on a flat surface. Standing far away from the painting, the effect one sees changes to that of a three-dimensional sculpture. What is amazing is that without wearing three-dimensional glasses, one can still very clearly see a three-dimensional effect.

The theme of this painting resembles seeing Mars through a telescope. The artistic clusters of yellow, red, black, and blue seem to have been created through the process of natural planetary erosion over millions of centuries. These colors exist in motion; they are constantly changing and transforming. In short, this painting will bring delight to those who view it.

Da Li Wang Zun Zhe
(Venerable Da Li Won) (#12)

Artist: H.H. Dorje Chang Buddha III
Style: Kuangxi

Venerable Da Li Won is a guardian deity of Buddhism who protects living beings and vanquishes demons. This is a painting of fine brushwork and close attention to detail. It is in the "Kuangxi" style. The bone structure, meridians, and veins of Venerable Da Li Won are visible. However, the technique used in this painting is different from the perspective technique used in oil paintings in that the scattered perspective technique used in Chinese paintings was applied. Extremely awe-inspiring in both spirit and form, Venerable Da Li Won is able to remove all evil hindrances and bless people with peace and health.

Portrait of a Lady
(#350)

Artist: Jean-Francois Portaels
(1818~1895)

Quite simply the most important Belgian painter of Orientalist subjects during the nineteenth century, Portaels was also a huge influence on a whole generation of Belgian artists. In this posed portrait, painted in 1870, we see the confidence he showed with his painting technique and his mastery of compositional balance.

Jean-Francois Portaels was born in the town of Vilvoorde in 1818 and as a boy of seventeen enrolled at the Academy of Brussels. There he was fortunate enough to be tutored by Belgium's greatest portrait painter, Francois Joseph Navez. From 1847-1849 he was Director of Painting at the Academy of Ghent, but by the winter of 1849 he had returned to Brussels. By then he had made the decision to spend much of his life in academia and, over the next forty years, held almost all of the major artistic posts in Belgium, including Director-General of the Academy of Brussels and President of the Royal Academy of Belgium.

He died in the small town of Saint-Josse-ten-Noode in 1895 but was given a State Burial in Brussels. His paintings are collected by many world famed museums, such as the Musee des Beaux Arts in Brussels, the Philadelphia Museum of Art in the United States, and others.

Shi Wai Tao Yuan
(Wonderland Beyond the World) (#104)

Artist: H.H. Dorje Chang Buddha III
Style: Chouxiang Yunwei

"Wonderland Beyond the World" is an ink-and-wash painting in the "Chouxiang Yunwei" style. The phrase "beyond the world" refers to the concept underlying the emotion and intrigue created by the brush strokes, which transcends conventional concepts of brush stroke technique by expressing an extraordinary emotional tone.

With a lively rhythm and bold flair, the limitless dynamism of the watery ink creates a wondrous effect that raises the work to a level of abstract artistry, rather than confining it to concreteness. The work aims not to portray objects precisely, but rather to convey the magical rhythm of objects. Through the charm of the dynamic watery ink, a sensory and spiritual pleasure is created. The power of the work's artistic spirit, rather than its colors and forms, guides the viewer's artistic enjoyment.

Interior with a Girl Knitting (#358)

Artist: Pierre Joseph Toussaint (1822~1888)

Usually working in a small format, Pierre Joseph Toussaint was a painter in the rich traditions of Flemish genre painting. His paintings frequently have an amusing quality in them, often depicting household staff at their chores. In this particular example, which can be dated to the 1870's, we see an interior scene with a young girl knitting. The artist has used this same interior in a number of other compositions but with differing figures within the paintings. The attention to detail that he brings to his work is nicely illustrated here as is the soft light effects that he had a predilection for using.

Pierre Joseph Toussaint was born in Brussels in 1822. At the age of fourteen he enrolled at the Academy of Brussels, where he was schooled in a traditionally Flemish manner. He remained there as a student and professor's assistant until 1850, when he left to establish his own career. Success soon followed and within a few years he was invited to exhibit at important salons in Brussels, Ghent, and Antwerp. His work was always well received and a number of them won significant prizes.

Pierre Joseph Toussaint died in Brussels in 1888. His paintings are in the collection of the famous Municipal Museum of Amsterdam, Netherlands and other museums.

18

Yun Shan Zhu Lou (#204) (partial picture)
(Bamboo Structures on a Cloud-Shrouded Mountain)

Artist: H.H. Dorje Chang
Buddha III
Style: Chouxiang Yunwei

This painting in watery ink features a gracefully charming scene in which the real and surreal coexist. It seems as if clouds and mist appear and vanish suddenly. Multi-level structures and a pavilion appear faintly in the mountain valley. This is a wondrous place of mountains inhabited by immortals and heavenly grass as beautiful as jade. Superior beings who have transcended this world reside in the lofty thatched houses made of bamboo. Impressively flowing, vibrant and ethereal, the ink seems to float about, having no fixed place. A marvelous tone flows through this image, like a heavenly song wafting through the cloud-shrouded mountains.

Xie Tuo Shan Chuan Fan Chen Qi
(Landscape Drawing Free of Any Mundane Tone) (#105)

Artist: H.H. Dorje Chang
Buddha III
Style: Wenfeng

By painting with the center-tip of the calligraphy brush as if writing calligraphy, the creator of this work portrays the states of both calligraphy and literature, displaying masterful skill in blending calligraphy with painting. The depth and charm of this natural work of art was created through the free and uninhibited state of mind of the artist.

This painting belongs to the "Wenfeng" style. This style has as its foundation traditional methods but has refined and transcended such methods.

Spirit (#52)

Artist: H.H. Dorje Chang
Buddha III

This work of calligraphy with the Chinese characters for "spirit" features the mature skills of a veteran calligrapher and understated charm. Its appearance lacks any trace of affectation and reveals an extraordinary calligraphic conception. There is no showiness to be found, no ostentatious air. The strokes appear steady and balanced, simple and unsophisticated. All forceful application of the brush was held back. The characters seem very plain but express a tone that is comforting, natural, and enjoyable. Every stroke is free from conventionality and has the natural look of a carving made by striking a chisel with a stone, or an image formed by broken roots from an old tree. Within this work of calligraphy, the extraordinary can be seen within the ordinary.

(#77)

20

Marvelous Charm (#77)

Artist: Yu Hua Shouzhi Wang

This flower looks simple but has clearly defined brush touches that are seasoned and natural. The flower stem, the three-dimensional feeling, and even the inscription all demonstrate the use of emptiness as form and the use of form to correspond with emptiness. The whole painting contains an atmosphere of marvelous charm. The lotus flower paintings of Yu Hua Shouzhi Wang (Dr. Yu Hua Wang) were praised in the United States Congressional Record as being unsurpassed in the history of Chinese art.

When Images of Three Buddhas Appear, the Genuine Nature of Jade Will Come Forth (#71)

Artist: H.H. Dorje Chang Buddha III

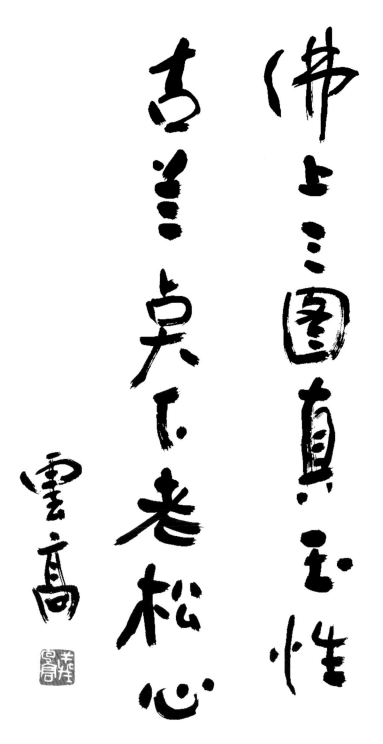

People regard jade as the treasure of all stones. Jade has the attributes of sleekness, brightness, firmness, non-deformation, colorful charm, steely strength, elegant beauty, and moistness. It has an air of unyielding integrity and is comforting to view. That is why jade is called the gemstone that represents purity and nobility. In particular, with the passage of time, jade looks purer and milder due to increased transparency. That is why jade is called the treasure of all gemstones. When offerings are made, jade is often offered as a symbol of loyalty.

This work of calligraphy was written by H.H. Dorje Chang Buddha III in Chengdu, China in the year 1990. Its meaning is that H.H. Dorje Chang Buddha III would appear in this world in the future when images of three Buddhas appear in the world; that is, when the lineage chart of H.H. Dorje Chang Buddha I, H.H. Dorje Chang Buddha II, and H.H. Dorje Chang Buddha III appears with their images.

The lineage chart of H.H. Dorje Chang Buddha III is worshiped in many Buddhist temples and other Buddhist sites all over the world. When those three images appeared, the true Buddha-dharma was like the nature of jade – unchanging – and it emanated the highest and purest fragrance and charm, like those of an ancient orchid. The true primordial, ancient Buddha stands upright like a lone pine tree and expounds the ultimate truth of tathagata-garbha to benefit all living beings. This work of calligraphy translates as, "When images of three Buddhas appear, the genuine nature of jade will come forth. An ancient orchid points to the mind of an old pine tree."

As predicted, the person formerly known as Master Wan Ko is the present day H.H. Dorje Chang Buddha III. This was affirmed by dharma kings, regent dharma kings, and great rinpoches of all major sects of Buddhism around the world, who wrote recognition certificates and corroborating congratulatory letters. This recognition of identity was indeed a grand event in Buddhism. The above-mentioned prediction made years ago in 1990 is truly wonderful beyond words.

22

(#56)

Wei Mo Shuo Miao Men (#56)
(Vimalakirti Expounds Wonderful Teachings)

Artist: H.H. Dorje Chang Buddha III
Style: Yousi

The elderly person in this painting called "Vimalakirti Expounds Wonderful Teachings" has a noble and sincere expression, an appearance that transcends the mundane, and an air of great compassion. One can easily see that He is definitely not of this mortal world. This virtuous being of utmost holiness is venerable Vimalakirti, one of the greatest and most famous persons in Buddhism. The depiction of Him in this painting is extremely lifelike. Even veins under His skin are visible. This painting is in the "Yousi" style. His serene face with a silvery beard, His demeanor of a Buddha, and His temperament befitting a great self-cultivator are all captured in the painting.

The painting demonstrates extraordinary artistic skills and conception and has a graceful arrangement. The whole work conveys a mind-purifying attractiveness. In short, it makes people feel at ease and comfortable. From the way the rock was painted, it is not difficult to discern the real proficiency and experience of the artist. It would be impossible for anyone who is not a great master of calligraphy to paint a scene that contains such natural charm, that is imbued with such a strong scholarly air, and that evidences such profound experience, nobility, and sincerity. It may seem that the rock and spring branches were casually painted with a small number of brush strokes. Actually, vast experience and profound calligraphic prowess were applied to depict them. Only through skills applied with a completely unfettered hand and mind can one reach this state of mastery in which calligraphy and painting merge.

The elderly person in the painting is the holy and venerable Vimalakirti, or Dorje Chang Buddha II, as recorded in Buddhist sutras. He is sitting near a rock expounding to living beings the dharma that He wrote. He is explaining that the best and highest Buddha-dharma is *The Supreme and Unsurpassable Mahamudra of Liberation*. As long as one cultivates oneself according to either one of the two dharmas of perfect accomplishment from *The Supreme and Unsurpassable Mahamudra of Liberation*, it will be very easy to liberate oneself from the cycle of reincarnation and become a holy person who has transcended the mundane world.

Lao Shu (Old Tree) (#6)
(partial picture)

Artist: H.H. Dorje Chang Buddha III

This ink-and-wash painting of tree trunks and plum branches suits both refined and popular tastes. The theme is elegant and graceful. The genuine-looking, lovely flowers exude a charming freshness. The old tree with its new branches and the real-to-life flowers with their attractive colors provide a distinct multi-layered feeling to this painting. Flowers at far and near distances look naturally different but do not appear stiff and lifeless. All parts of the scene form a harmonious whole that people can appreciate without end.

南無觀世音菩薩

(#14)

24

Na Mo Guan Shi Yin Pu Sa (#14)
(Prostrate to Guan Shi Yin Bodhisattva)

Artist: H.H. Dorje Chang Buddha III
Style: Yousi

Guan Yin Bodhisattva is a Bodhisattva at the level of marvelous enlightenment, which means possessing the marvelous enlightenment of a Buddha. That is, the Bodhisattva is one of great holiness and virtue who is no different from a Buddha. As recorded in sutras, Guan Yin Bodhisattva is the incarnation of an ancient Buddha called True Dharma Brightness Tathagata and is the king of great compassion. The Bodhisattva is incessantly busy day and night helping all humans and other living beings in the Three Spheres and has accumulated boundlessly vast merit. This painting was created in the year 1980. In creating this work, the artist adopted the style of the ancient murals inside the Dunhuang Grottos in China in charm, spirit, overall appearance, and lines. This painting belongs to the "Yousi" style.

Xia Jiang Yao Du
(Ferrying the Xia River)
(#16)

Artist: H.H. Dorje Chang Buddha III
Style: Fanjuan

"Ferrying the Xia River" is an ink-and-wash painting created in 1993. Although black ink is used extensively, the brush strokes contain the essence of the art of painting and calligraphy. Even though the only color used is black from top to bottom, the aspects of farness and nearness are clearly distinguishable. A top artist, Mr. Huang Binhong, said "Black ink is all around, as extensive as heaven and earth. The paper of a painting can unfurl thousands of mountains. Created with ease in less than a few days, this work was actually born from nearly one hundred years of wielding the brush." This painting has a rich layered look. Within the thick black ink lies elegance. It is an excellently conceived and interesting image. In this leisurely and carefree setting, sounds echo from thatched cottages amid mountains to skiffs on the water and vice-versa. This remarkable work with an exceptional style and scholarly air is one of the paintings in the "Fanjuan" style and was created using the center brush-tip technique.

Mei Lin Yi Jiao
(Corner of a Plum Blossom Grove) (#5)
(partial picture)

Artist: H.H. Dorje Chang Buddha III

This painting of a scene from nature realistically portrays an enlarged corner of a plum blossom grove.

Yellow plum blossoms bloom in winter and are generally used during Chinese New Year celebrations as a symbol of great auspiciousness. The artist's skillful wielding of the brush created a painting that expresses and even surpasses the beauty of a real plum blossom grove. This work of art is even more enchanting than a true plum blossom grove and provides a refined aesthetic enjoyment that brings comfort to the mind.

Hao Duan Ru Sheng
(Brushwork that Has Reached a Holy State) (#17)

Artist: H.H. Dorje Chang Buddha III

This landscape painting was created with masterful calligraphic touches of the brush. At first glance, the image appears somewhat although not totally chaotic, for there is also order amid the chaos. However, when this painting is carefully viewed, one will see why it is a masterful work of perfect order in which all parts interconnect. Some scenes seem to be so afar. Even the closer roads seem to lead to faraway places. Charm is expressed through the proper balance of dense and light tones and haziness. The high artistic state of depicting a painting through calligraphic skills is fully exhibited. A few huts embellish multipeaked mountains. Profound mystery is secretly hidden in this brushwork. The grand style of this painting is totally free from mere conventionality. The huts were created from just a few casual strokes, yet they seem to enhance the lovely sentiments expressed by every grass and tree in the painting.

Portrait of an Elegant Lady Holding a Fan (#351)

Artist: Jean-Baptiste-Siméon Chardin (1699 ~ 1779)

Jean-Baptiste-Siméon Chardin was an 18th century French painter. He is a master of still-life and is also noted for his genre paintings that depict kitchen maids, children, and domestic activities. Carefully balanced composition, soft diffusion of light, and granular impasto characterize his work. Chardin was born in 1699 in Paris to the family of a master-carpenter. In 1724 Chardin was accepted into the Academy of St. Luke, a rival to the Royal Academy, though lacking the latter's royal patronage. In 1728, Chardin submitted two of his famous paintings to the Royal Academy and was accepted and made Associate and Academician, which was quite a rare achievement for any artist, let alone one who had not actually studied at the Academy.

This superb eighteenth century French portrait retains an old frame and bears a plaque ascribing the painting to Jean-Baptiste-Siméon Chardin. Although portraits of this type by Chardin are rare, this painting bears marked similarities to genre works executed in the mid to late 1730's. Chardin's works are collected by a number of world-class museums, including the Musee de Louvre in Paris and the Pushkin Fine Arts Museum in Moscow.

Gu Bo Yin Quan
(Ancient Cypresses and a Murmuring Spring) (#202)

Artist: H.H. Dorje Chang Buddha III
Style: Wenfeng

The basic style of this artwork is a traditional scholarly style found in Chinese paintings based upon the artist's talents and learning. This painting belongs to the "Wenfeng" style. One can clearly see that extremely seasoned and mature brushwork skills were used and that this painting reflects the profound learning of a scholarly artist. The lofty mountains, murmuring spring, and ancient cypresses as dark as black dragons were essentially completed from top to bottom in one color – black. However, various levels of nearness and farness, an air of sedateness, and a natural charm are manifested.

Female Study (#365)

Artist: Carolus-Duran (1837~1917)

This sensational study of a young girl from behind dates to 1888, which was considered by most to be the artist's most important period. Presented in its original frame, it perfectly encapsulates Carolus Duran's love of painting the female form. He was born Charles Emile Auguste Durand on July 4th 1837 in the northern French town of Lille.

Carolus-Duran studied drawing at the academy in Lille with the sculptor Augustin-Phidias Cadet de Beaupré, but by the age of 15 had begun an apprenticeship in the studio of François Souchon. After moving to Paris in 1853, where he took classes at the Académie Suisse, Carolus-Duran quickly made the acquaintance of a number of his artistic contemporaries, including Fantin-Latour, Courbet, Manet, and Monet, with whom he would establish life-long friendships.

He is today universally regarded as one of the foremost and most influential French academic painters of the nineteenth century. When he died in Paris on February 18th 1917, the whole country mourned his passing. His paintings are collected by major museums throughout the world, such as the Louvre in Paris and the Metropolitan Museum of Art in New York.

Bi Shang Zhi Gong
(Skillful Brushwork) (#30)

Artist: H.H. Dorje Chang Buddha III
Style: Fanpu

This painting was created in 1982 during the time a film was being shot in Sanhe, Sichuan. It is an on-the-spot painting of a real-life scene. Ink was used sparingly, as if it were as precious as gold, yet the artist's skills are demonstrated. At that time, the News Film Studio of China was shooting a documentary exclusively about the artist Wan Ko Yee.

The cameramen and others present saw a wild duck alight upon a withered tree trunk. Wan Ko Yee immediately lifted His brush and promptly finished the entire painting. By the time the wild duck raised its wings and flew away, the painting had already been completed. Moreover, the artistic prowess this artwork embodies is extraordinary. It not only perpetuates the elegance, purity, and high-quality of traditional paintings, it also expresses a new style. People who saw Wan Ko Yee create this painting were greatly surprised. They highly praised Him for having artistic skills and conceptions resembling but surpassing those of Bada Shanren (a famous Ming Dynasty painter). They also highly praised Him for His scholarly style that even excels the scholarly style reflected in ancient stone seals. At the time, the artist Wan Ko Yee was still in His early youth and was praised in the newspapers as a young hero. However, people did not know then that Wan Ko Yee is H.H. Dorje Chang Buddha III, as we now know.

This painting is in the "Fanpu " style.

Xiang Tu Qing Nong (Heartwarming Countryside) (#11)

Artist: H.H. Dorje Chang Buddha III

"Heartwarming Countryside" was conceived by H.H. Dorje Chang Buddha III based on His highly seasoned and mature painting techniques yet was painted with the naturally innocent mindset of a child. It is a painting but does not look like one. Beauty and elegance are hidden within simplicity. The emotional appeal of this countryside village is quite thought-provoking. Although it may appear that a child wielded the brush to create this painting, it was actually created through highly developed, mature artistic skills and a mind free of attachment. The picture comes from real life but surpasses real life. The mountains, waters and land reflect the elevated state of the artist – non-attached, free, and unconcerned. However, this casualness reveals the artist's all-encompassing breadth of mind. Fascinating aspects of this painting are hidden deep within it.

Noble Manner (#51)

Artist: H.H. Dorje Chang Buddha III

The two Chinese characters in this work of calligraphy mean "Noble Manner." They manifest a calligraphic style that is different from other styles in the world. The artist created this work of calligraphy free of any mental attachment or artificiality and without any pre-existing calligraphic plan or intent. His writing hand was unfettered, and his heart was free. All movements of the brush were spontaneous. Natural charm that springs from childlike innocence was attained. This type of impromptu wielding of the brush can be described as the cursive writing style of a child. The term "Noble Manner" means that one should have an elevated and broad manner, an all-inclusive magnanimity. We should let others, rather than ourselves, have that which is beneficial so that we may attain a noble moral character, and we should cultivate a mentality of non-attachment in order to develop our virtue.

A Lotus Pond Has
Carp (#135)

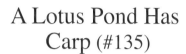

Artist: H.H. Dorje Chang Buddha III

The title "A Lotus Pond Has Carp" suggests profound philosophical implications that transcend everyday life. In addition to its masterful artistry, the painting contains subtle messages of the Dao and its fruits. The lyrics on the left and right sides of this work correspond perfectly with the image of the fish, forming a whole that awakens and enlightens, richly rewarding its viewers.

Why is this painting so artistically enchanting that it stirs the hearts of those who see it? One reason is that the fish are depicted with uncanny realism. The swimming carp are infused with vitality. The painting's details clearly reveal damage done to the carp's skin, accumulated over a lifetime in the water, through lines that fade in and out. Appearing as delicate as fine gauze, the translucent fins, for example, possess

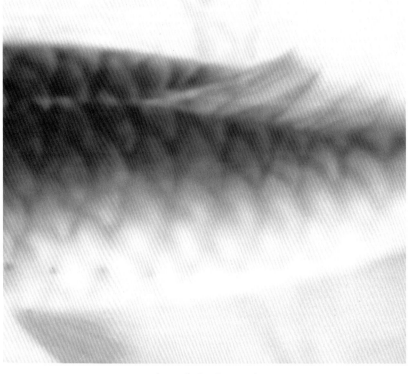

(partial picture)

a natural realism. Texture and spirit are captured with utter precision, providing the viewer with stirring aesthetic pleasure. The surface and bottom of the pond are depicted with a wonderfully hazy charm, while the lotus flowers, leaves, and pods are portrayed in bold freehand brushwork with distinct and unusual brush strokes rapidly applied.

The painting is mainly composed of black ink and rich colors. Only a few brush strokes were used to create each vibrantly red flower, which seem to emit a pure fragrance. The hanging lotus pods embellish the painting, conveying an elegant contrast of hues and instilling a sense of vitality. As the fish swim about, free of any inhibition, the sunlight faintly reflecting off the water ripples provides the illusion of movement that occurs in the natural world.

When examined more closely, the painting has a style that is difficult to ascertain, for it seems to transcend realistic fine brushwork but also seems to convey the feeling of freehand brushwork. It is not in the style of conventional paintings. Rather, freehand brushwork was applied to produce the effect of fine brushwork with close attention to detail. Fine brushwork was applied that actually transcends realism. The real and the surreal commingle, resulting in a work that excels the beauty of a natural lotus pond. It represents a combination of techniques from the "Menglong" style of painting, as well as bold, large-scale freehand brushwork.

Although both are paintings of fish, this work and the marvelous "Dragon-Carp Playing in a Lotus Pond" a painting with carp and lotus pond by the same artist, possess entirely different wondrous appeal, reflected in their lotus leaves, flowers, and pods. For example, the lotus leaves in "Dragon-Carp Playing in a Lotus Pond" possess an elusive, abstract charm, while the ones in this painting are portrayed in a bold, direct manner. To say this painting's direct portrayal merely lies in its powerful, bold strokes, however, would not suffice. More accurately, it should be described as possessing a strong and penetrating spirit with a charm that is completely free and unrestrained. This is a painting deserving of the following words used to describe Chinese paintings of the highest level: "The whole scroll may appear messy, as if it was smeared by the golden paws of a flying dragon; yet, what appears chaotic is not in disorder, for there is a soaring charm that is inexhaustibly beautiful."

The other painting, "Dragon-Carp Playing in a Lotus Pond," lies at the other end of the artistic spectrum. Each of the two paintings represents the best of their respective styles. The lotus leaves and flowers in "Dragon-Carp Playing in a Lotus Pond" were depicted in watery ink and look soft, moist, fragrant, and natural. That painting's wondrously charming, vibrant, and extremely elegant leaves and flowers seem to be in a constant state of change. Together, they carry the viewer into a world of wafting fragrance.

Both paintings contain lotus leaves, flowers, and pods. However, one painting possesses a strong tone, as if muddy dragons rolled wildly across the scroll, as well as an aggressive, sharp tone. Conversely, the other painting embodies the loftiness of a divine dance amidst the clouds and the purity and elegance of jade. The perspective of this comparison, however, is merely one of artistic appreciation.

Upon encountering the title of this painting, "A Lotus Pond Has Carp," those with superior understanding will immediately recognize that it points to the wonderful essence and profound meaning deeply embedded in the painting. The mention of carp is not simply to indicate that the lotus pond contains carp but rather to indicate that the painting contains the Dao. The painting's extraordinary artistry, which is completely devoid of any trace of the mundane, mysteriously reveals the true face of holy wisdom. The Dao hidden in this painting is not that which ordinary people can understand.

H.H. Dorje Chang Buddha III composed these lyrics of a Dao song for the painting: "No Dao exists on the high mountain, yet hearts yearn to go there. A lotus pond has carp; men have inquired about them. Which path leads to the truth is worth pondering. It would be better to look tranquilly to our original nature, like a lotus flower tranquilly sitting over its leaves." These lyrics speak of mysteries unknown to the common person – seeing fish not as fish; seeing water not as water; no Dao exists on the high mountain, so no value exists in searching for it; and the fish have neither life nor death.

To understand the origin of the painting, we must ask where the fish came from. What state of realization was relied upon and gave birth to this exquisite painting? What state of realization manifested this mysterious, hazy, and illusory painting? The magical illusion of the fish and water is nothing more than a superficial image. Spirit is within. A life-force underlies spirit. Sprit is empty, or nothingness. The original essence of all things is that which is neither empty nor substantive. Everything illusory and impermanent quickly changes in time and space, but their original nature remains constant. Thus, the lyrics of the Dao song continue: "To find our original nature, do not seek the source, as the source is our original nature, tranquil and unmoving, like a lotus flower tranquilly sitting over its leaves. That is, there is no such thing as arising, passing away, and change. From this surpassing wisdom, usages that arise from Buddha-nature will naturally manifest. These usages include calligraphy and painting. Only in such a way is a consummate work created." Thus, one should understand the wonderful meaning of this song of Dao written on this painting. Profound mysteries are deeply hidden within it.

In case the viewer remains oblivious to this first stanza, the second stanza of the song continues with: "The carp rely on the Dao, and the Dao awakens the fish." The Dao refers to the state of holy ones, a realm that transcends the realm of ordinary people. It does not refer to ordinary abilities. This painting of carp was created on the basis of such a holy state. "The Dao awakens the fish" means that this painting of carp in a lotus pond was accomplished based on the wisdom of the transcendent Dao. Only with such wisdom could this lifelike, graceful scene of carp swimming in water be painted, a scene that combines the real and the surreal, emptiness and substance in such a wondrously appealing way. This scene of carp complimented by the boldly and powerfully depicted lotus leaves is the result of the artist's awakening to the holy Dao.

This painting of carp, then, is merely an expression of one who has attained the Dao and reached enlightenment. Thus, this work is not just an ordinary combination of brush strokes, color, ink, and water. Rather, it is the result of techniques derived from the wonderful application of holy wisdom. The profound mysteries contained in "A Lotus Pond Has Carp" cannot possibly be conveyed by the superficial meaning of the words in its title! Actually, this explanation is completely unnecessary. All those with discerning eyes will understand once they see the lyrics of the Dao song and the calligraphic skills with which they were written on the painting. That is because this painting of carp that contains an accompanying Dao song is the work of H.H. Dorje Chang Buddha III—the work of a Buddha.

32

(#8)

Shu Hua Zhen Yuan (True Source of Calligraphy and Painting) (#8)

Artist: H.H. Dorje Chang Buddha III
Style: Wenfeng

This painting called "True Source of Calligraphy and Painting" was inscribed with the name "Wan Ko Yeshe Norbu" also known as H.H. Dorje Chang Buddha III. It was painted in Los Angeles, California and clearly reveals the artist's talent. Mastery is found in each brush stroke. The artist's profound and extensive erudition and calligraphic skills permeate the painting. Free from worldly conventions and devoid of garishness, this work engenders its own style of painting called the "Wenfeng" style. It points out the path leading to the true source of calligraphy and painting. The entire painting is filled with an air of scholarliness.

Three Beautiful Flowers of Clear and Extraordinary Charm (#74) (partial picture)

Artist: Yu Hua Shouzhi Wang

When commenting on lotuses painted by Yu Hua Shouzhi Wang, the first thing to mention is the intoxicating atmosphere she produces through every application of watery ink. Her usage of brush and ink to depict the spirit and form of lotuses entails numerous unexpected variations. She naturally intermingles separation and unity, restraint and boldness, realism and surrealism.

These buds that have not yet blossomed forth thoroughly evidence her transcendent skills in painting lotuses. It is in the style of large-scale freehand brushwork using the splash-ink technique, She has adopted the ancient style of refined simplicity and added to it her own innovation, resulting in such fascinating, vivid, lifelike, and natural brushwork. This magical artistic treasure came from real life but transcends real life. It is named "Three Beautiful Flowers of Clear and Extraordinary Charm."

Mysteries of Zen (#85)

Artist: H.H. Dorje Chang Buddha III

These two characters whose meaning is "Mysteries of Zen" are in the running script style. Written in a free and easy manner, they embody natural grace, dignity, poise, and profound inner power. The exquisite signature "Dorje Chang Buddha III" corresponds perfectly with the main body of the calligraphy and presents a consistently well-structured attractiveness. The meaning of these two characters is that Zen contains profound mysteries, and within these mysteries is profound meaning. To enter Zen is to penetrate these mysteries without attachment. In the state of Zen, one is in a boundlessly vast world.

(#13)

Gu Tu (Native Land) (#13)

Artist: H.H. Dorje Chang Buddha III
Style: Chouxiang Yunwei

"Native Land" belongs to the "Chouxiang Yunwei" style of painting of H.H. Dorje Chang Buddha III. Inner-restraint of the artist marks the brushwork of "Native Land." This painting has a noble, classic, and powerful look to it. One can easily see that the rock in the picture is the place where giant mythical birds and mighty eagles circle and dwell every day. The visible bird droppings that still remain on that rock are those of mighty eagles that dwelled there over a long period of time. The rock looks like a cultural relic and is in different shades of color, from light to dark. It obviously appears to have existed over a very extended period. There is much residual matter on its surface. It is easy to see that this is the residence of the king of birds, a place with an imposing air of might that definitely keeps all other beasts, birds, and fowl from daring to invade.

The arrangement of this painting and the techniques used evidence artistic experience and unadorned simplicity. Charming appeal and the painter's artistic conception can be found within simple ordinariness. This work of art expresses a grand vision and is devoid of any sign of rashness on the part of the artist. It also conveys the profound thought that one will not be attacked by evil forces only if one possesses outstanding, imposing, and extensive virtue.

This is the original, authentic painting. Another one that appeared in some books is a duplicate of this painting. At the time the authentic painting was created, Master Wan Ko thought that inscribing His calligraphy on it would not be appropriate. Therefore, He kept this excellent work and did not wield His brush to inscribe it until 2010. The painting is inscribed in Chinese with its name, "Native Land," and the name of the artist, "Dorje Chang III." It is stamped with the three-dimensional, eight-jewel, gold-inlaid fingerprint seal as proof that it is the authentic original painting. This original painting is much larger than the duplicate, as the duplicate was only around eighteen square feet.

Ancient Withered Vines Become a Fossil Fortress (#83)

Artist: H.H. Dorje Chang Buddha III

"Ancient Withered Vines Become a Fossil Fortress" is the name given by H.H. Dorje Chang Buddha III to a Yun sculpture. The style of this calligraphic work was also created by H.H. Dorje Chang Buddha III. It is highly elegant and has an appealing scholarly air. The calligraphy seems to consist of broken bamboo slips. The thickness of each stroke and the structure of each character are just right. Emptiness and substance complement each other, producing a graceful appearance. However, this form of calligraphy is very difficult to learn. It requires the fusion of skills and naturalness. Only with a holy and pure mind can one accomplish such phenomenal brushwork.

36

Niu Nian Tu (#32) (Year of the Buffalo)

Artist: H.H. Dorje Chang Buddha III   *Style: Fangfa*

"Year of the Buffalo" was created in January of 1985. Here the artist used the scattered perspective technique to give a three-dimensional appearance. Emptiness was used to depict form. Form and emptiness blend into one. The layout of this painting is highly elegant. It is a work of art that conveys natural charm and reflects an innocent, childlike mind, thereby providing people with comfort and enjoyment. What is particularly marvelous is the application of ink on a minute level to depict the hairs of the oxen in countless variations. This boundlessly fascinating and enchanting creation is in the artistic style of "Fangfa." What was published in earlier years was printed from a duplicate of this painting. The inscription on the duplicate is "Year of the Buffalo, spring of the year Yichou, Zhi Wan Yee." It was not until 2010 when the genuine original painting became known to the world, inscribed with the words "Year of the Buffalo, Dorje Chang III."

Hibiscus and Carp (#261) (partial picture)

Artist: Guo Ruyu
Style: Chinese ink-and-wash painting in fine brushwork

Professor Guo Ruyu was born in China in December of 1941. He is a member of the Artists Association of China. His positions include Director of the Creation and Research Department of the Sichuan Province Poetry, Calligraphy and Painting Institute; President of the Chengdu City Fine Brushwork Painting Association; Dean of Chengdu Fine Brushwork Painting Academy; and Dean of Sichuan Province Oriental Painting Art Academy.

Paintings of hibiscus and carp by Guo Ruyu are representative of his paintings. They are also the works that established his reputation. Such paintings have been collected and exhibited by many important organizations in China, including exhibition in the Great Hall of the People in China.

Guo Ruyu meticulously created this painting specifically for this museum. Without even the slightest trace of water seen on or near the fish, a sense of fish swimming and moving about in water is depicted. This special characteristic of Oriental art whereby the artist conveys a concept, such as water, without painting it is fully manifested in this painting. The extremely simple brushwork that was used to paint the carp portrays their very rich texture. With careful observation, viewers can experience the boundless appeal of this artwork. This painting is truly representative of the art of Chinese painting.

(#64)

38

Ke Yan Zhan Bu (#64)
(Viewing the Waterfall Flowing Down Shell Rocks)
(partial picture)

Artist: H.H. Dorje Chang Buddha III
Style: Miaoxie

The brush touches in this painting are unfathomably wondrous and vary unpredictably. They bring forth limitless allure. It is a painting of scenery using watery ink and minute freehand brushwork, yet the realistic effect of fine brushwork is manifested. Why does this painting appear to have been done in fine brushwork yet was actually done in freehand brushwork? You will discover after careful examination that it was completely painted in freehand brushwork rather than fine brushwork.

In this delightful image, the variations and interplay among the many brush touches are deftly and naturally portrayed. What appears chaotic is not in disorder. Every touch of the brush was casually applied. This lovely brushwork has transcended the mundane and is free of all gaudiness. A particularly wonderful feature of this painting is that the color white is manifested through contrast with black rather than through the usage of white paint. Black and white are so intermingled, they form one inseparable whole. The effect of fine brushwork is manifested through minute freehand brushwork. A strong scholarly tone of superb quality is produced at the level of minute details.

The painting depicts ancient rocks and caves formed over millions of years through geological and weathering processes. The waterfall looks as though it was created by nature itself. This work is in the "Miaoxie" style of painting.

Yi Mu Shan Zhuang (#179)
(Mountain Village with Memories of Mother)

Artist: H.H. Dorje Chang Buddha III
Style: Xiangtong

In creating "Mountain Village with Memories of Mother," the artist maintained a childlike, innocent mind, while wielding the brush with an experienced, mature hand. A calligraphic style was used. The brush was steered by the wrist and driven by the force of the arm with utter spontaneity. Completed in a free and uninhibited manner, this piece was not painted for the sake of painting. The application of ink and colors is totally natural.

What is art? To put it simply and straightforwardly, art is the ability of a creation to immediately inspire mental or spiritual ease, comfort, satisfaction and enjoyment within its viewers. From what is this enjoyment derived? Is it the contents of the artwork? Take painting, for example. Does a painting become a good work of art simply because its images are aesthetically pleasing? This is absolutely false. The contents of a painting are not the critical element. Instead, in the terminology of Chinese painting, the key is that elusive experience of the painting's spiritual resonance. It is a vivid yet nebulous and intangible quality; it is an enchanting spiritual power that cannot be articulated through words. It occurs when the artist's masterful state of artistry and personal cultivation seeps into the work, creating a powerful charm and allure.

Only after experiencing this spiritual resonance do viewers begin to study the painting's contents, its colors and arrangement, its brush stroke techniques and use of ink, its degree of capturing the subject in spirit or in form, its composition, its balance between calligraphic writing and painting, and so on.

In reality, whether a Chinese painting is good or whether it truly inspires a sense of comfort is not determined by the artist's technique. Instead, it hinges upon the painting's ability to inspire spiritual resonance. That is the true essence of art. "Mountain Village with Memories of Mother" indeed possesses this artistic spirit. It enchants the viewer's mind and spirit with its ink brush strokes. This work of art belongs to the "Xiangtong" style of painting.

39

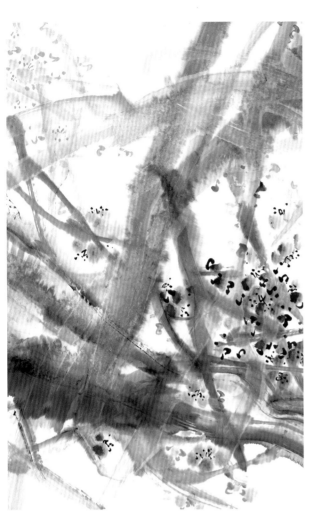

Sheng Jing Mei Xiang Han Yun Nong (#68) (partial picture)
(Fragrant Blossoms and Strong Wintry Charm Born of a Holy State)

Artist: H.H. Dorje Chang Buddha III
Style: Fanpu

This painting is in the "Fanpu" style. The brushwork, casually applied, was accomplished with an unfettered hand and detached mind, free of the slightest artificiality. The conception behind the layout was not based on optimizing the overall appearance of the painting. However, one can instantly see that everything painted is both abstract and realistic. It is a seemingly ever-changing work. Its charm, tone, transitions, and depictions represent the highest level of Eastern ink-and-wash paintings. This artwork fully deserves to be called a magical creation captivating in both spirit and form and full of unexpected transitions. From these exceedingly beautiful transitions comes an allure whose source is the power of the spirit of life.

Thoroughly examine this painting and you will see that it truly is superb. A transparent layer of lighter ink on top of darker ink is clearly visible, imbuing the painting with a pure and fragrant air and providing the viewer with a feeling of comfort and ease. To paint such a painting, the artist must possess solid calligraphic skills and be able to tap into a foundation of profound and extensive knowledge. He must let go of any mental attachment to self or ego when wielding the brush. He must abandon all attachment to an inherently existing self and apply brush to paper in a spontaneous, unimpeded manner. Only then will he be able to create this type of a wondrous painting through a state of non-attachment.

A Hidden Wonderland (#46)

Artist: H.H. Dorje Chang Buddha III
Style: Menglong

"The remotest corners of the earth are still part of the human world. Those who search for the truth in their dreams perceive themselves as wise, virtuous persons. To find out through which mountain pass you can leave this dusty world full of impediments, look for the cave hole with remnants of light, for that will lead to the Land of Peach Blossoms."

H.H. Dorje Chang Buddha III wrote this poem containing a profound message in order to express the true meaning of this painting: Nowhere in this human realm can one find a place not of ordinary people, not of this mundane world. All born as human beings are in a dream of confusion. However, they usually believe they are seeking the truth. In reality, they are just indulging in self-appreciation and self-consolation. As such, they cannot block the great flow of impermanence. However, there is one opportunity whereby you can attain control over your own living and dying and be guaranteed to transcend this world of mortals. When you see the wondrously intriguing cave hole with remnants of light, know that is the source you are seeking. That is the paradise of immortals, the Land of Peach Blossoms, a holy land beyond this world.

The style of this painting is Western oil painting plus a mysterious technique that combines the dual skills of fine brushwork and freehand brushwork. From the harmonious unification of these three elements, a holy land of immortals with an unusual landscape of inexhaustibly beauty comes into being. It is as if the viewer is taken to a palatial cave, to a world of no worries, and is looking over this wonderland that is beyond our world. The marvelous variations in color, light, and atmosphere are so enchanting that the viewer is carried away to that place, fascinated in the loveliness of it all. This painting belongs to the "Menglong" style of painting.

Le Retour du Troupeau (#338)

Artist: Louis Aimé Japy (1840~1916)

A student of François Louis Français and of Camille Corot, Louis Aimé Japy made his Salon debut in 1864, during the height of the Barbizon movement. He made trips to Italy early in his career, as was customary for a young artist, but it was the regions of his native Doubs and the Jura that most captured his heart; these regions inspired most of his compositions. Japy exhibited his views of the French countryside regularly at the Salon, receiving a medal in 1870, earning a second-class medal in 1873 and gold medals at both of the Expositions Universelles in 1889 and 1900. In 1883, he was made a member of the Société des Artistes Français, earning him exemption from all future Salon jury selection and the ability to exhibit freely at the Salons. He was recognized again in 1906, when he was elected Chevalier de la Légion d'Honneur.

Japy's works of art have been collected by many world known museums, such as the Louvre in Paris and the Rijksmuseum in Amsterdam.

Shuang Ying Heng Shi (Two Eagles on a Flat Rock) (#208)

Artist: H.H. Dorje Chang Buddha III
Style: Chouxiang Yunwei

The style of this painting, "Two Eagles on a Flat Rock," is a combination of charming appeal and vigorous brushwork. Such a style belongs to the "Chouxiang Yunwei" style of painting. The approach was to alter the true appearance of the two gallant eagles yet capture their spirit. Reality is depicted in a non-real manner. Forms are portrayed in an altered way. In his use of brush and ink, the artist emphasized a quality of powerfulness throughout the painting. Charm is seen from the mixture of realism and surrealism and from the vigorous tone. The artistic conception upon which this painting is based came from an ordinary scene in nature.

(#69)

Small Delightful Autumn Scene (#69)

Artist: Yu Hua Shouzhi Wang

When people highly praise paintings or calligraphy, they almost always crown such works with aesthetic terms such as "fine and concise use of brush and ink," "vividly charming," or "vigorous and graceful." Actually, such descriptions aptly describe the spirit and appearance of this painting. The layout is neither too wide nor too narrow and encompasses neither too much nor too little. The charm of color is enhanced through empty space. A delightful scene is produced from these mutually complimentary elements of color and emptiness. Watery ink was used to depict the emotional appeal of this painting. Artistic variations in heavy and light hues can be found in every part of the painting. It is a very natural and vigorous looking painting that is devoid of any mediocrity. The tone of the ink seems to be ever-changing, appearing both dense and thin. There is a definite attractiveness arising from the varying degrees of haziness. In short, it is a joy to behold!

Yu Hua Shouzhi Wang has attained consummate mastery in the field of lotus flower paintings, surpassing all others both ancient and contemporary. This conclusion was recorded in the United States Congressional Record when a special exhibition of her works of art was held at the United States Capitol in November of 2008.

Hao Duan Zan Zuo Gang Dao Feng, Dian Ran Dan Qing Shu Juan Nong (#206)
(My Brush Produces the Effects of a Carving Knife Without Losing a Strong Scholarly Effect)

Artist: H.H. Dorje Chang Buddha III
Style: Banqi

At first glance, this painting looks like an engraving. However, after careful observation, that conclusion will be completely overturned. You will discover that fine and meticulous painting is deeply embedded within the knife-like brush strokes. Moreover, with variations of dark and light hues, brushwork that evinces a natural and free mentality can be seen everywhere. Besides being completely devoid of any trace of the mundane, this painting displays the childlike mindset of the artist. This painting embodies extraordinary artistry because it was created with a brush yet exhibits carving skills! It is in the "Banqi" style of painting.

Gao Jie Tu (Noble and Pure) (#44) (partial picture)

Artist: H.H. Dorje Chang Buddha III   Style: Pomo Weiyun

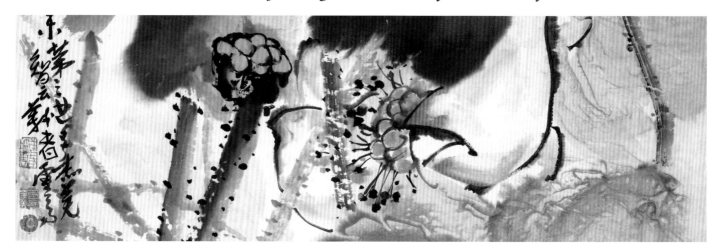

It can be said that this painting, "Noble and Pure," is a masterpiece among lotus flower paintings. Flowing splash-ink on the scroll produces a vivid charm that evidences great ingenuity. There is an air of power and grandeur together with elegance. With absolutely no trace of stiff, common, mundane artistry found in other lotus flower paintings, this work of wondrous charm is free from worldly conventions and devoid of garishness. Indeed, it exemplifies a state of holiness. The artistic conception and brushwork are absolutely flawless, which make it a work of unsurpassed quality. The inscription on the painting reads, "Look, the charm has blossomed forth. What need is there to paint the details?" Just from reading the inscription, one can understand how consummate the artistic skills of H.H. Dorje Chang Buddha III are. The style of this painting is "Pomo Weiyun."

Stone Seals (#47)   *Artist: H.H. Dorje Chang Buddha III*

Engraving stone seals, calligraphy, and painting are indivisible parts of one whole. If an artist does not know the art of calligraphy, his paintings will lack a scholarly air. If he does not know the art of poetry, his paintings will not reflect literary skills. If he does not know the art of engraving stone seals, his paintings will not exhibit the charming jagged look of inscriptions on ancient stone seals.

That is why H.H. Dorje Chang Buddha III stated, "Poetry, calligraphy, painting, and stone seals can be traced to the same origin and are in the same strain. The truth of this good lesson from the ancients should be practiced. A general review of famous artists from ancient times to the present points to a fact. If one does not have other-worldly methods and only concentrates on a single artistic subject, regardless how he practices or how he researches the essence of his artistic subject, his attainment after several decades may still be nothing but superficial and insignificant. I occasionally looked at the methods and accomplishments of the famous painters Baishi, Changshuo, and Bada Shanren. Such an experience made me realize that wondrous artistic appeal originates from excellence in all those fields. How can any one of those fields be isolated from the others?..."

The overall meaning of the above inscription on this work "Stone Seals" is as follows. Literature, calligraphy, and engraving stone seals are one indivisible entity. This is the conclusion the ancients reached long ago based on experience. A sweeping view of famous Chinese painters from antiquity to the present reveals that not even one of them became a master painter without great skills in all three fields. Of course, this refers to true masters of art, not painters who have an undeserved good reputation.

This work called "Stone Seals" manifests the brimming talent of H.H. Dorje Chang Buddha III in His early years. However, people may not know that the engraving of stone seals is only a very small part of the infinite wisdom of today's H.H. Dorje Chang Buddha III. After reading the book *H.H. Dorje Chang Buddha III*, one will understand that engraving stone seals is merely one of the thirty categories of accomplishments exhibited in that book. Moreover, the entirety of those thirty categories of accomplishments still constitutes only a very small portion of the wisdom and accomplishments of H.H. Dorje Chang Buddha III. He possesses great wisdom that is difficult for ordinary people to imagine. His accomplishments are all real, and His good reputation is definitely deserved.

Town Scene with Figures (#364)

Artist: Jan Hendrik Verheyen (1778~1846)

As a painter of pure town-scenes, Jan Hendrik Verheyen had few equals. His extraordinary attention to the minutest of details made his work so sought after during his lifetime that he could barely keep up with the demand. He was born in the Dutch town of Utrecht on December 22, 1778 to a family of merchants. Around 1820 he turned his attention to painting the street scenes of Utrecht, the works that would become synonymous with his name. During that period private collectors were keen to acquire the town scenes of the seventeenth century masters Gerrit Adriaensz, Berckheyde and Jan Van der Heyden, but because of the huge sums involved few collectors could afford these works. This gave the opportunity for artists such as Verheyen to produce works of a similar vein to satisfy such demand.

Verheyen enjoyed an illustrious career, exhibiting throughout the Netherlands at numerous important art venues. He died in his home town of Utrecht on January 14th 1846. His works are collected by many well known museums, including the Palais Des Beaux Arts in Brussels, Belgium, the Stedelijk Museum in Amsterdam and many other museums.

Still-Life with Roses (#353)

Artist: Achille Theodor Cesbron (1849~1915)

Achille Theodor Cesbron was born in Oran, Algeria in 1849. His career really began in 1877 when he was first invited to show at the prestigious Paris Salon. His skills as a painter were recognized by the judging committee of the Salon, who awarded him an honorable mention in 1882, Bronze medal in 1884 and Silver medal in 1886. He was also awarded a silver medal at the 1889 World Fair in Paris. When he won the Legion of Honour in 1897, this award was handed to him by William Bouguereau, France's greatest painter of the nineteenth century.

He was an expert in flower painting, renowned for the fineness and sensuality of his floral compositions and particularly for his ability to represent roses. He was commissioned, along with his friend and contemporary Georges Jeannin, to decorate the *Salon du Passage* at the City Hall of Paris. His love for art and horticulture led Cesbron in 1902 to found the flower garden in the city of Paris at the Porte d'Auteuil.

His works are collected by numerous famous museums, including the Musée d'Orsay in Paris, the Municipal Museum of Fine Arts in Chateaudun, and museums of other countries.

Ba Shan Xiao Jing (Small Scene on Mount Ba) (#108)

Artist: H.H. Dorje Chang Buddha III
Style: Xiangtong

In this work, the strength of the brush is so powerful that its strokes seem to have been carved by a knife. The artist created this painting in a completely free and unfettered state of mind. It is not a painting created for the sake of painting, but rather a painting that emerges from calligraphic writing. There is a flavor and spirit that leaves the viewer with the impression that this work is composed of randomly applied strokes created with a totally unattached mind. Actually, the brushwork is rigorous and tidy, as well as delightful in its seeming clumsiness. This painting belongs to the "Xiangtong" style.

Langga Luobu
(Treasure of Heaven) (#84)

Artist: H.H. Dorje Chang Buddha III

This calligraphy is truly very beautiful. Even minute traces remaining after a stroke of the brush have special appeal. At an exhibition displaying the art of H.H. Dorje Chang Buddha III held in the United States Capitol, this calligraphy was exhibited along with the work of art it names. It is in one of the calligraphic styles of H.H. Dorje Chang Buddha III derived from the childlike style and the running script style. Anyone who understands calligraphy knows that it is extremely difficult to imitate this style. One must possess profound knowledge and cultivation as well as a solid foundation in stone inscriptions. Otherwise, one could not possibly attain such a level of brushwork mastery. "Langga Luobu" means treasure of heaven.

Wei Zhen (Majesty) (#58)

Artist: H.H. Dorje Chang Buddha III   Style: Kuangxi

Various techniques were used in this painting entitled "Majesty" in order to enable viewers to see clearly the fur of this gallant lion and his cubs. Brush touches of various degrees of thickness and thinness were applied. Stone-based coloring material used in Chinese paintings was also applied. Every stroke of the brush became a separate hair. The process required much labor. Such a painting takes one to two years to complete. In short, a long time and painstaking effort are needed.

The mighty lion in this painting is in a lying pose with a majestic, awe-inspiring appearance that shakes the skies and land. Large-scale freehand brushwork was used to paint the rock and trees in the surrounding scene. The versatile skills of the artist are fully evidenced. The brushwork was completed in a mature, vigorous, bold, and spontaneous way. Naturally imbued in this surrounding scene are the profound literary and other talents of the artist. Painting mastery was reached in depicting this very appealing surrounding scene in which what appears chaotic is not in disorder and what appears somewhat real is abstract. Experts in calligraphy can see that each brush stroke used to paint the huge rock on which the lion lies was applied with a free and unfettered hand. Calligraphic skills were used with the effect of painting. Painting skills were used to bring out the spirit of the work. Brush techniques were applied to express charm and power. Calligraphy and painting unite in this one work of art. This artistic treasure contains energetic strokes and embodies a grand artistic conception. Its style belongs to the "Kuangxi" style of painting.

Gang Gu Sheng Feng (partial picture)
(An Air of Unyielding Strength) (#4)

Artist: H.H. Dorje Chang Buddha III

The title of this painting, "An Air of Unyielding Strength," indicates its style, emotional appeal, and skillfulness. This painting matches its title. Every brush stroke shows the skill of the artist. The bold and forceful style of stone inscriptions can be seen in the crisscrossing of twigs, branches, and tree trunks. Although red plum blossoms created through light touches of the brush are numerous, they are not randomly arranged, for there is order within apparent randomness. This painting originates from real life yet transcends real life. Its plum blossoms surpass real plum blossoms in beauty and in conveying the uplifting notion of bravely withstanding the snowy winter.

This work of art is an enlarged re-creation of an earlier painting by Wan Ko Yee Yeshe Norbu with an almost identical name. It was inscribed with the Chinese characters for Dorje Chang III and was also stamped with the three-dimensional, eight-jewel, gold-inlaid fingerprint seal as proof of its authenticity.

Lan Se Bing Tian
(Landscape of Icy Blue) (#213)

Artist: H.H. Dorje Chang Buddha III

From the blue charm of an ink-and-wash painting, it is not difficult to see the level of an artist's accomplishment and talent. This painting called "Landscape of Icy Blue" may seem simple. However, after one attempts to copy it, one will know how deep it truly is. The mountains and trees were painted in the same watery ink color as the sky. Wondrous charm flows within the surreal depictions. The attractive theme and colors fuse naturally into an integral whole. Each touch of the brush was applied without the slightest mental attachment. The artist's mind captured the spirit of the painting, which is manifested in the image. One can see the distinct differences between dense ink and light coloring, all accomplished without any sign of artificiality. The interplay of the real and the surreal together with unexpected variations produce a charming effect throughout the entire painting. This artwork provides the viewer with aesthetic enjoyment due to its free, other-worldly, dreamy tone.

Ducks in a River Landscape (#341)

Artist: Leon Germain Pelouse (1838~1891)

Born in 1838 in the small town of Pierrelaye within the Val d'Oise area of Northern France, Leon Pelouse was to become one of the most highly respected landscape painters in nineteenth century France. After becoming a professional artist, he moved to Paris, where he established a studio and in 1865 commenced exhibiting at the Paris Salon. His beautiful views in the Normandy and Brittany areas of France were soon gaining him a reputation. He came to the attention of the Rothschild family, who commissioned him to paint a number of works for their magnificent house at Veux-de-Cernay.

Throughout the 1870's and 1880's, his work was regularly winning medals and prizes at the various important salons of the time. The bestowment of the Legion of Honour for his services to French art was the high point of an exciting career. Leon Pelouse died in the town of his birth in 1891, but his works are collected by museums throughout France, including the Musee d'Orsay and the Musee de Luxembourg in Paris. Other world museums that own paintings by Pelouse include those in Belgium, Switzerland, Canada, Germany, and Australia.

This superb example of his work dates to around 1880 and typifies his fresh approach to the painting of landscapes.

Can Qiao Ting Tao Sheng (Listening to the Rushing Brook from a Dilapidated Bridge) (#216)

Artist: H.H. Dorje Chang Buddha III

The brush touches in this painting may appear to be chaotic but are not. Watery ink of various shades was applied, producing the commingling of the real and the surreal. The brushwork is so subtle one can see variations of the real and surreal in every stroke. None of the strokes are stilted. The painting has a scholarly tone and an air of unevenly graceful stone seal engravings. Flowing, graceful brushwork of watery ink is revealed even amid bold and vigorous brushwork.

Although this is a small-scale painting, it displays excellent, seasoned artistry. Whether it be the houses, the dilapidated bridge, the rushing brook, or the noble people on the bridge, all of them were painted in a spontaneous manner with no pre-planned artistic conception. Everything was painted in an utterly natural way. As these two verses state, "The artist's mind contains broad knowledge found in the books of myriad schools of thought. With effortless facility, he creates an elegant image."

Full-Length Portrait of Captain Barneby (#369)

Artist: Sir Martin Archer Shee (1769~1850)

He was born in Dublin, of an old Irish family, but Martin Shee nevertheless studied art in the Dublin Society and came to London. There in 1788, he was introduced by William Burke to Joshua Reynolds, on whose advice he studied in the schools of the Royal Academy. He was chosen an associate of the Royal Academy in 1798, and in 1800 he was made a Royal Academician.

Shee's portraits were in league with such contemporaries as Thomas Lawrence, John Hoppner, Claude Phillips, Jackson and Henry Raeburn. The earlier portraits of the artist are carefully finished, easy in action, with good drawing and excellent discrimination of character. In addition to his portraits, he executed various subjects and historical works.

In 1830, Shee was chosen president of the Royal Academy, and shortly afterwards he received a knighthood. Shee's artwork is collected by many world renowned museums, such as the Metropolitan Museum of Art in New York and the Royal Academy Collection in London.

This portrait of Captain Barneby, when he was still a young man, shows him in the uniform of the Grenadier, or Senior, Company of the Hereford Militia.

Repos du Bétail (#339)
Artist: Rosa Bonheur (1822~1899)

Rosa Bonheur's first teacher was her father; she later became a pupil of Léon Cogniet. At a young age she showed an extraordinary talent for drawing people and animals, outlining them with great skill. She also showed an independence of mind and strong will from an early age; she ran away from school and then from a workshop where she was apprenticed, declaring that she wanted to be an artist. She overcame her father's opposition to the idea and persevered. She undertook her first studies in the Bois de Boulogne, which was still fairly wild in her youth. At this time, the French philosopher Félicité Robert de Lamennais (1782-1854) and the author George Sand both had a decisive influence on freeing her from prejudicial thinking. She wore men's clothes to visit local slaughterhouses and fairs and mingled with horse-dealers and cattle men. She first exhibited at the Salon of 1841 with two animal paintings. At the next exhibition, alongside her paintings, she exhibited a terracotta sculpture of sheep. At the 1843 exhibition, in addition to paintings, she sent a plaster sculpture of a bull.

In 1843 she won a third-class medal. She won a first-class medal in 1848 with *Ploughing in the Nivernais,* and it was clear that her talent was fully mature. At the Salon of 1853, she exhibited *Horse Market* which, popularized by an engraving, placed her among the foremost painters of her time. She was made a Chevalier of the Legion d'Honneur in 1865 and an Officer in 1894. She was also a Commander of the Order of Catholic Isabella and the Order of Leopold of Belgium. She was a great friend and protegee of Queen Victoria, which made her works much sought after by the British aristocracy.

Bonheur was a serious artist who devoted the whole of her life to her work. At the end of her brilliant career, she changed her palette entirely to give her works the powerful coloration of the Impressionists. In 1997 the Musee des Beaux-Arts, Bordeaux mounted a retrospective exhibition of her works, which traveled to the Dahesh Museum in New York in 1998. In 2001 some of her sculptures were included in the exhibition held at the Musee des Arts Decoratifs, Bordeaux *(Around Barye and Pompon - Animal Sculptures of the 19th and 20th Centuries).*

Her works are collected by numerous world famous museums, such as the Metropolitan Museum of Art in New York and the Musee d'Orsay in Paris.

(#57)

Bei Shang Dong Zhi
(Wintry Branches in the North) (#57)

Artist: H.H. Dorje Chang Buddha III
Style: Menglong

Paintings people commonly see are Chinese paintings, Western paintings, ink-and-wash paintings, watercolor paintings, oil paintings, prints made from an engraved plate, and so on. They definitely have not seen a painting in this style. This fascinatingly charming technique created by H.H. Dorje Chang Buddha III is that of the "Menglong" style. Moreover, it is an artistic style that harmoniously fuses ink-and-wash painting, engraved plate printing, oil painting, and other techniques. The artist seeks to capture unusual loveliness within the seemingly usual and seeks to convey a sense of beauty from unexpected transitions of style. Ice and snow were not piled up in this painting to create an icy and snowy scene. Rather, a chilly, frosty scene is conveyed without explicitly visible accumulated snow. With the addition of a few earthen houses with reddish walls, the unadorned wintry scene of a countryside village in northern China appears vividly on paper. The viewer is instantly transported there and, being affected by the tranquility of this northern countryside, feels completely open and at ease.

Hun Hou Hua Zi Shu Juan Nong
(Rich, Thick Ink Displays Profound Learning) (#33)

Artist: H.H. Dorje Chang Buddha III
Style: Wenfeng

This landscape painting entitled "Rich, Thick Ink Displays Profound Learning" is in the "Wenfeng" style. Looking at its content, one can see that the application of brush to paper reflects the same touches and brushwork found in calligraphy. The viewer can immediately see very solid, traditional artistic skills as well as a scholarly tone that pervades the entire painting. A charm suggestive of both calligraphy and poetry is contained within this one painting, thereby demonstrating a high degree of artistry.

From the brush strokes, details, and color, one can see that the real is hidden within the surreal, the surreal is revealed from within the real, and what appears chaotic is actually not. This is exactly what is meant by the saying, "Seen from near, it appears chaotic. Seen from afar, one discerns a myriad of mountains and an elegant chaos that reveals ingenuity and profundity." When viewed from a close distance, the image appears confusing, as if it is just a flat scene without any nearby rocks or remote mountains. However, when viewed from a far distance, the image is extremely clear. The various layers of depth become obvious. Far away and nearby mountain ridges, terraces, and paths become extremely clear. Standing at a distance of about thirty feet, the viewer can truly recognize the essence and charm of "Rich, Thick Ink Displays Profound Learning."

View of a Riverside Town (#362)

Artist: Johan Hendrik Van Mastenbroek (1875~1945)

Johan Hendrik Van Mastenbroek was born in the Dutch town of Rotterdam in December 1875. His father, the painter Johannes Van Mastenbroek (1827-1909), was his first teacher and recognized his latent, precocious talent.

His paintings reflect the subtle light of the Netherlands, and his depictions of busy port and canal scenes are amongst the finest of his day. His reputation as an artist soon spread internationally, and by the late 1890's he was winning awards and medals throughout Europe. For his services to Dutch art, he was awarded a special gold medal by Queen Wilhelmina of Holland. After a long and illustrious career, Johan Hendrik Van Mastenbroek died in the town where he was born on November 16th 1945.

This particular work by Mastenbroek dates to his finest period and was included for exhibition in the extensive retrospective held at the Kunsthal Museum in Rotterdam in 2004. Paintings by Van Mastenbroek are held in museum collections throughout the world, including the Musee de Louvre in Paris, the Rijksmuseum in Amsterdam and many others too numerous to list.

Si Yu Sheng Hui (#91)
(Resplendent Like Jade) (partial picture)
Artist: H.H. Dorje Chang Buddha III

There seems to be a common belief in painting circles that paintings of plantain trees and lichees are easy to paint. However, this painting in front of you is by no means easy to paint. How could a work of ordinary appeal deservedly use the title "Resplendent Like Jade"? The natural-looking, pleasing plantain tree in this painting was drawn with only a small number of strokes. It is so beautiful and pleasant, so elegant and enrapturing. It appears so natural, without the slightest mark of artificiality. The plantain leaves were painted vigorously and spontaneously. Each of the elegantly simple and adeptly painted matching lichees was completed with just a small number of brush touches. Both the plantain tree and lichees lack any mediocrity and were painted without the slightest mental attachment in the mind of the artist.

The key point is that, with just a small number of simple strokes, the whole painting is impressively imbued with a strong jade-like charm and an auspicious air. This is aptly expressed in the following short poem: "Unfurl the painting scroll and the especially fragrant scent of ink is sent forth, permeating the viewer's mind and intoxicating him to the core. No more than a small number strokes were applied. This is the king of paintings in which ink is used as sparingly as gold."

Da Mo Zu Shi (#9) (Patriarch Bodhidharma)
Artist: H.H. Dorje Chang Buddha III

This painting in the freehand brushwork style was created from only a small number of brush strokes. Through the artist's seasoned adeptness and uninhibited brushwork, this painting embodies the natural essence of all things. The subject is Bodhidharma, a Patriarch of the Zen Sect of Buddhism. This painting expresses the original nature of Zen, which neither arises nor passes away, abiding imperturbably. Artistry devoid of the slightest affectation shows the natural ease with which the artist wields the brush when creating calligraphy

and paintings. Actually, this is the essence of Zen, the truth of the universe, naturalness that is free of attachment.

The Kui Gate (#228)

Artist: H.H. Dorje Chang Buddha III

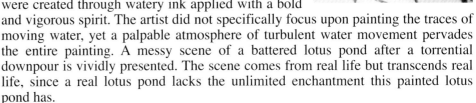

"The Kui Gate" is located at the Three Gorges in Sichuan, China. This calligraphy is a poem written by H.H. Dorje Chang Buddha III in the 1980s when He was traveling along the Yangtse River through the Three Gorges. He passed through the Kui Gate to the City of Baidi. That day He composed one hundred poems on the spur of the moment. "The Kui Gate" is one of those poems and translates as, "Beyond the narrow pass of The Kui Gate, the city of Baidi hangs above. From green flowery waves emerge one hundred poems. Writings cannot outlast water speeding eastwardly. Heroes of heavily contested battles are now nothing more than mud statues." This poem of four seven-character verses speaks of the truth of impermanence in this human world.

This work of calligraphy is devoid of any trace of artistic immaturity or superficiality. The skills of a veteran calligrapher were employed in an unfettered, spontaneous, unattached way. It was written casually, without any artificial embellishment. As such, it reveals the true source, the nature of the mind. The style resembles that of a mischievous child joyfully playing with a brush. This work of calligraphy reflects the ability of the writer to return to the mindset of a child. That is why this script is called "the child script." This is the most difficult calligraphic style. It entails a childlike tone yet exhibits skillfulness born of inner-attainment. This naturally requires reaching a state of realization in which a mature, experienced adult regains the heart of a child.

Yu Hou (After the Rain) (#61)

Artist: H.H. Dorje Chang Buddha III
Style: Pomo Weiyun

"After the Rain" exemplifies the "Pomo Weiyun" style of painting. The spirit and form of the subject portrayed through this technique are especially intriguing. The application of watery ink displays unpredictably: there is order in the midst of chaos and the juxtaposition of abstraction and realism. It is an inexhaustibly alluring work with marvelous, soothing appeal. Amid myriad lotus leaves, a single lotus flower blooms near a lotus bud tinged with soothing red, providing for a refreshing, invigorating scene. Each lotus stalk was completed with one stroke of the brush without any touchups to augment their visual appeal, yet the natural texture of the stalks is captured. The stalks are crisscrossed, standing upright, leaning horizontally, broken, bent, or lying on the ground. Water drops leave traces of their slow path down the lotus leaves.

Such striking liveliness and mesmerizing charm were created through watery ink applied with a bold and vigorous spirit. The artist did not specifically focus upon painting the traces of moving water, yet a palpable atmosphere of turbulent water movement pervades the entire painting. A messy scene of a battered lotus pond after a torrential downpour is vividly presented. The scene comes from real life but transcends real life, since a real lotus pond lacks the unlimited enchantment this painted lotus pond has.

This is the original "After the Rain" painting. Years ago a duplicate version of the same size appeared in some books and albums of paintings. A replica made from this original was photographed and then printed and published in those books and albums. However, the inscriptions are different. The inscription on this original painting is "Dorje Chang III," and it is stamped with the three-dimensional, eight-jewel, gold-inlaid fingerprint seal. The duplicate has the inscription "Zhi Wan Yee" and does not contain a fingerprint stamp.

Bao Shou Tu (Precious Animals) (#59)

Artist: H.H. Dorje Chang Buddha III

The first feeling you have when looking at this painting is a strong sense of comfort and a natural and tranquil enjoyment. At this moment, you forget everything else, focusing all of your attention on the painting. Why? It is not the allure of a typical painting of pandas. Rather, it is the embodiment of the highest accomplishment in the art of painting – riveting charm and elegance together with a pure and extraordinary resonance.

This painting of five pandas is a rare and precious work of art. Its layout harmoniously integrates emptiness and form, fully expressing a pure and fascinating appeal. The method applied by the artist combined the scattered perspective technique used in Chinese paintings with the logical three-dimensional spatial perspective used in Western paintings. The pandas were painted in fine brushwork, reflecting meticulous attention to detail and realistically capturing the vividness of their fur. In addition, the style of freehand brushwork was used to paint the surrounding trees and scene. The splash-ink technique applied to depict the surrounding scene provides a charming air of liveliness. This vivid combination of the surreal and the real makes this a painting of wondrous brushwork.

With the two techniques of fine and freehand brushwork cohesively fused, this piece is totally free of mundane artistry commonly found in the surrounding scenery of panda paintings. This painting exhibits a scholarly style befitting a master of art. A sense of stiffness or rigidity typical of works by common artists is completely absent.

We often see that paintings of pandas in fine brushwork inevitably contain some degree of mediocrity and unoriginality. Moreover, the fur of the pandas often conveys a sense of uncleanliness. Such brushwork does not express an air of freshness and purity that transcends the mundane. Why? The problem lies with the inability of such artists to depart from mediocrity in their techniques and frame of mind. That is because they do not possess scholarly knowledge and have not studied the four forms of Chinese poetry, the Chinese classics, history, and the commentaries. Thus, the surrounding scenes that they paint tend to reveal a mundane quality.

Conversely, the surrounding scenes of this panda painting are truly unique. The artist portrays the vividly charming artistic essence of dual styles and three-dimensional space. The pandas are more beautiful than real ones and even better-looking and more lifelike than photographs of pandas. They exemplify utter beauty, elegance, purity and cleanliness, as if they had just bathed in pristine water.

This composition is in the style of "Kuangxi."

Zhong Sheng Yin Yin
Chu Lin Jian (#214)
(The Sound of Bells Faintly Echo through the Forest)

Artist: H.H. Dorje Chang Buddha III
Style: Fanjuan

This painting was created through the technique of calligraphic writing and the addition of details and colors. It has a deep scholarly tone reflective of the profound learning of the artist. We can see the mood and charm that are expressed through the brush. For instance, the trees and the mountain are almost one indistinguishable entity. The mountain is the trees, and the trees are the mountain, with waters and rocks interspersed here and there. The whole scene is full of spots, but what may appear chaotic is not in disorder. The entire setting exudes a sense of comfort and naturalness.

To sum up in one sentence, the maturity of an artist is based upon profound and extensive knowledge. Those who are apt to boast of themselves but who lack real abilities do not even come close to such maturity. What is this painting? It is the crystallization of inner-cultivation, virtue, and knowledge.

Summer Landscape with Figures by a Farmhouse (#345)

Artist: Karl Schultze (1856~1935)

Karl or Carl Schultze was born in Dusseldorf in 1856 and became one of the finest landscape painters of his day. He received his training at the Dusseldorf Academy under the direction of the Head Professor of Fine Arts, George Oeder. It was Oeder who not only taught him the fundamentals of painting but also instilled within the young artist a love of painting pure landscapes. Graduating around 1880, he commenced his career as a professional artist and established a studio in Dusseldorf. Although he was based in his hometown, many of his paintings depict scenes in other areas of Germany, particularly the Alps, for which he seems to have held a special fascination.

His paintings were highly prized during his day and were frequently exhibited at the principal German exhibition venues to great acclaim by the public and critics alike. After a long and successful career, Karl Schultze died in Dusseldorf in 1935. His works are collected by the famed Braunschweig Museum in Dusseldorf, Germany and other museums.

This example of the work of Karl Schultze dates to 1882 and can be regarded amongst the artist's most important works. Surrounded by its magnificent original frame, it perfectly encapsulates Schultze's predilection for painting scenes bathed in a cool light with a tremendously close attention to detail.

Interior Scene (#348)

Artist: Dirck Wyntrack (before 1625~1678)

It is not known with any certainty when and where Dirck Wyntrack was born. His dated works are from the period 1642-1670. Wyntrack had concentrated on the representation of entvogelen (the seventeenth-century Dutch word for duck and other waterfowl), and there were very few artists as skilled at it as he. He died in 1678 at his house on Delft Wagenveer in The Hague.

The present painting, deaccessioned from the Los Angeles County Museum of Art, is a magnificent depiction of a kitchen in a barn interior. His composition is dynamic, an extensive still-life including at the forefront kitchen utensils, copper pots, wooden barrels, various root vegetables, two goats, a dog, and plates of fish, rendered in an opaque palette in Wyntrack's precise, painterly style.

Works by Dirck Wyntrack are collected by many famous museums in different countries, including the Los Angeles County Museum of Art and the Museum Bredius, Hague.

Tao Hua Shan Zhuang Zhi Long Tan Hu
(Dragon Pond in Peach Blossom Mountain Village) (#86)

Artist: H.H. Dorje Chang Buddha III
Style: Pomo Xiantiao Xiezhen

This is a real-life portrayal of Dragon Pond in Guanxian, Sichuan. Techniques from the "Pomo Xiantiao Xiezhen" style of painting were used to compose this painting, which contains realistic mountains, water, clouds, and mist. It seems that the storm dragon is about to emerge, for the land, water and sky share a similar tone. At that time, it was about to rain. Dense mist envelopes the area and dark clouds hang in the sky, giving the scene a rather strong emotional appeal and a very stirring atmosphere. The splash-ink technique was applied to bring out the charm of this painting, and the center brush-tip technique was applied to draw the lines that make up the vivid scenery. The image is both realistic and artistic, reflecting skills in both large-scale splash-ink and meticulous brushwork. It is a thought-provoking landscape painting that nurtures the mind and spirit.

Ruins - Palenque, Yucatan (#346)

Artist: Charles Dorman Robinson (1847~1933)

Born in Maine, Charles Dorman Robinson's parents moved to California in 1850 when he was three years old, and he grew up in San Francisco. At thirteen he was awarded a diploma by the Mechanics' Institute for best marine drawing. He was recognized as a first-rate marine painter in 1878, when he won all the prizes at the Sacramento State Fair. One picture was even purchased by Governor Booth.

In the 1870's new ideas from Europe were being introduced. One of these was the plain air technique that gave artists the freedom to explore the atmospheric effects of light and color. Robinson's preference was for the luminescent quality of early morning or fading light, and in RUINS-PALENQUE he captures the mystical softness of the decaying ruins.

Robinson was in Paris for the 1900 Exposition, where one of his paintings was purchased by a British noble. It was later presented to Queen Victoria, who hung the picture in Buckingham palace. One of his works was also acquired by the King of Siam during a visit to San Francisco. Tragically, many of Robinson's works were destroyed in the 1906 San Francisco fire, and in 1921 a fire at his Laguna Street home took twenty years of his Yosemite paintings.

Robinson, together with Jules Tavernier (1844-1889), was co-founder of the Palette Club in San Francisco. His works are collected by museums such as the De Young Museum in San Francisco and the Crocker Museum in Sacramento.

Xi Shuang Ban Na (#75)
(partial picture)

Artist: H.H. Dorje Chang Buddha III

This is a Chinese ink-and-wash painting of fine brushwork. However, it has a three-dimensional feeling suggestive of oil paintings. The first version of it was just a quick sketch made by H.H. Dorje Chang Buddha III in Xi Shuang Ban Na, Yunnan Province. After He brought it back to Sichuan, He completed the painting with fine, delicate, meticulous brushwork.

In order to achieve charming, harmonious coloring that provides a sense of comfort and warmth, He chose light brown as the main color. There is also fresh, clear water and misty air circling between the trees. As an additional embellishment, a few girls of the Bai nationality are making waves, chatting, and enjoying themselves as they wash clothes by the riverside. Cobblestones are naturally scattered in the water at different depths near the riverbank. The setting resembles an illusion or a place described in a poem. The local conditions and customs of Xi Shuang Ban Na, a small portion of a large territory full of beautiful mountains and rivers, seem to appear before our eyes in this painting in fine brushwork.

To Shine Like the Sun and Moon, Cultivate Peacefulness by Being Tolerant and Patient (#263)

Artist: H.H. Dorje Chang Buddha III

This work of calligraphy translates as, "To shine like the sun and moon, cultivate peacefulness by being tolerant and patient. To last as long as the mountains and rivers, be a benevolent one of virtue." This couplet was written by H.H. Dorje Chang Buddha III to masters who learn and practice Buddha-dharma. It encourages those masters to lead well the Buddhist practitioners who follow them. Only by acting in accordance with what is written in this couplet can one become a noble person.

The meaning of this couplet is as follows: No matter what our circumstances may be, we must always remember to be tolerant and patient under insult and adversity and cultivate our conduct at all times. Additionally, we should broadly plant seeds of goodness and develop ourselves to be selfless people of noble moral character. This type of morality is as bright as the sun and moon. Those who personify it will receive the respect and love of others.

"To last as long as the mountains and rivers, be a benevolent one of virtue" refers to people who have a noble moral character; who exemplify benevolence, justice, proper manners, wisdom, and faithfulness; who show loving care for others; and who selflessly contribute to others. Their state of realization and virtue will last as long as the mountains and rivers, never fading away.

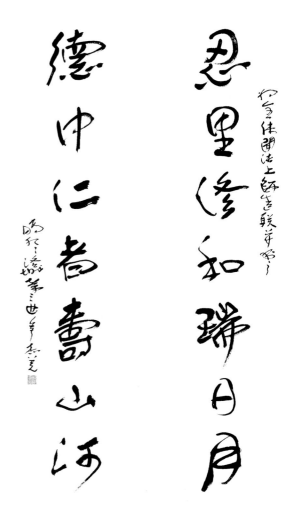

(#38)

Qiu Se Yan Yun
(Mist, Clouds, and Autumnal Color) (#38)

Artist: H.H. Dorje Chang Buddha III
Style: Pomo Weiyun

"Mist, Clouds, and Autumnal Color" is a splash-color painting that conveys a very strong sense of flowing watery ink and colors. An air of power and grandeur expressed through clouds that seem to swallow mountains and waters pervades the entire painting. The natural, captivating charm of this scene is similar to the charm of a scene on the ground after a long, flowing river has just rolled by. This setting is embellished with red maple leaves and houses amid autumnal, cloudy mountains, presenting a wonderful image distinctly characteristic of fall. When carefully examining the watery ink that produced such charm, one can see beautiful areas that are themselves paintings within a painting and details that are hidden within rough brushwork. Even within small areas are subtle variations of darkness and light, of the surreal and the real, all the while embodying splendid charm.

This painting is one of the representative splash-color works that H.H. Dorje Chang Buddha III created in His youth. It belongs to the "Pomo Weiyun" style of painting. Very tiny signs of charm can be seen amid this large-scale splash-ink painting. Soaring charm and exceptional beauty are words that aptly describe this work. The original version of this painting contains the inscription "Mist, Clouds, and Autumnal Color; Dorje Chang III" and is stamped with the three-dimensional, eight-jewel, gold-inlaid fingerprint seal. There also exists a duplicate that is generally the same as the original. That duplicate contains the inscription "Mist, Clouds, and Autumnal Color; Zhi Wan Yee" but does not contain the fingerprint stamp.

Mu Mian Shuang Chu
(A Pair of Chicks Under a Bombax Flower Tree) (#62)

Artist: Yu Hua Shouzhi Wang

Two exuberant chicks are playfully vying with each other. The brushwork style is simple, clear, and free of mediocrity. A natural charm is expressed. Several simple brush strokes evince mature, experienced, vigorous artistry. The large amount of space that is left blank in the painting forms an attractive and relaxed style in which the blank paper is part of the painting and emptiness expresses color. Light touches of the brush depict red bombax flowers. Only one flower is needed to convey a touch of loveliness. This painting also contains the artist's signature and a seal stamp. The overall layout of this work is exceedingly elegant and refreshing. Each brush stroke of this extremely exquisite creation adds to its natural attractiveness. This artistic treasure in which ink was used sparingly exemplifies a high achievement in Chinese painting.

Chan Sheng (#212)
(The Sound of a Cicada)

Artist: H.H. Dorje Chang Buddha III
Style: Wenfeng

This painting depicts a real scene from life using a casual painting method that captures the natural feel of the scene. The brushwork expresses a cultured, scholarly tone as well as a lively, spirited charm. A cicada in cold weather is perched high upon a thick branch. The image is so lifelike and natural. The cicada was painted in fine, delicate brushwork. The key to the appeal of this artwork is that it was painted in a casual manner yet is natural-looking and lacks any trace of the mundane.

We can see from this painting that the artistry of H.H. Dorje Chang Buddha III matured very early. Although He created "The Sound of a Cicada" in His early years, seasoned and vigorous brushwork skills are vividly presented.

Auspicious Atmosphere of a Lotus Pond
(#73) (partial picture)

Artist: Yu Hua
Shouzhi Wang

This painting displays the auspicious atmosphere of a lotus pond through bold and vibrantly charming brushwork. Leaves appear separate from one another but actually may not be. Shapes appear realistic but actually may not be. The scene may appear chaotic, but actually is not. There is a strong sense of fluidity. The arrangement is grand. Water and ink blend harmoniously. This painting is totally devoid of any artificial touch of the brush or sign of mediocrity. People can enjoy the dynamic charm that exudes from the entire painting. Just from looking at the flowers one can sense the amazing dexterity that produced such wondrous enchantment. The brushwork is clean, graceful, seasoned, and vigorous. The form and spirit of this elegant scene are captured. The commingling of the real and the surreal is masterful, natural-looking, and aesthetically pleasing.

Tiny (#53)

Artist: H.H. Dorje Chang Buddha III

The meaning of these three Chinese characters is as follows. Regardless of how great one's abilities are, even if one's talents are unsurpassed in the entire world or one is the leading authority in a certain field, as a human being, one should develop one's virtue, build one's true abilities, and benefit others. To do this, one must first be modest and open-minded and regard oneself as a very ordinary person, a servant to others, a tiny, insignificant being. One should not think that one is superior to others in any respect. Only by considering the interests of others in such a way can one become selfless and be naturally magnanimous.

This work of calligraphy was created with an artistic mind. It is free of any mental attachment and was written spontaneously rather than with a purposeful, thought-out calligraphic plan. However, just from looking at each stroke, one can clearly see that the artist's calligraphic skills have reached a high level. The artist has attained the superb state of being able to return to the mindset of a child. This is a special ability whereby the artist maintains a childlike, innocent mind yet wields the brush with an experienced, mature hand.

Winter Landscape with Skaters (#357)

Artist: Cornelis Lieste (1817~1861)

Born in Haarlem in 1817, Cornelis Lieste can be counted amongst the top painters of the Dutch Romantic School. His small, delicate winter landscapes remind one of the works of Leickert and Schelfhout. His paintings are tightly detailed and enjoy a bright and cheery color palette. As a young man he took studies with Jan Reekers and Nicolaas Roosenboom, where he learned the traditions of Dutch Realist painting.

His qualities as a painter soon became apparent and, along with his contemporaries Rochussen, Sande-Bakhuzen and Verboeckhoven, he was at the forefront of mid-nineteenth century Netherlandish painting. In 1840 he continued his studies in Belgium and then in Germany before returning to Holland in 1841. In 1842 he was invited to show at the prestigious Felix Meritis exhibition in Amsterdam, where he was awarded a gold medal for a landscape work. From 1854-1856 he lived in the town of Oosterbeek, and it is works from this period that are most highly prized by collectors.

His later years were spent actively in painting, but he died at the young age of 43 in the town of Haarlem in 1861. His paintings, drawings, and prints are collected by a number of important museums in the Netherlands and other countries, including the Rijksprentenkabinet Museum in Amsterdam and the Teylers Museum in Haarlem.

Thatched Stone Huts on a Snowy Mountain (#276) (partial picture)

Artist: H.H. Dorje Chang Buddha III
Style: Weiyin

This painting evokes an open feeling of ease upon first glance. In that initial moment, it seems one does not discover anything specific in the painting. As the colors of black, white, green, and red give rise to a sense of comfort, the spirit of the painting slowly emerges.

Only upon closer examination of the charm and sentiments conveyed by the painting does one discover that it seems to portray a lofty space, high in the universe. Thatched stone huts appear faintly on the plateau of the cliff. They resemble the homes of gods. The more one views this painting, the more one is able to sense its refreshing qualities of elegance and purity. This is a painting in the "Weiyin" style.

The Water Carrier
(#347)
Artist: Daniel Ridgway Knight
(1839~1924)

The Water Carrier, executed with rich color and detail, is a charming example of landscape and portraiture, the genre for which Daniel Ridgway Knight was best known. The peasants of France were his favorite subjects. Most popular were his paintings of peasant girls, alone or in pairs, with their wooden shoes and picturesque clothing, at work, in conversation or personal reflection. Story-telling pictures of peasant life were much in vogue in Paris, and his work was sought after on both sides of the Atlantic.

Daniel Ridgway Knight was born in Philadelphia and attended classes at the Pennsylvania Academy of Fine Arts along with Mary Cassatt and Thomas Eakins. Later, he settled in Paris, where he spent most of his life. He exhibited regularly at the Paris Salon, also sending his paintings to the United States for exhibitions at the Brooklyn Academy and the National Academy of Design. He was the recipient of numerous medals and honors throughout his career, including the coveted Medal of Honor from his Alma Mater, the Pennsylvania Academy of Fine Arts.

Works by Daniel Ridgway Knight are collected by many museums, including the Pennsylvania Academy of the Fine Arts and the Georgia Museum of Art in Athens.

Seen at Yellowstone National Park (#280) (partial picture)
Artist: H.H. Dorje Chang Buddha III   Style: Weiyin

The colors of this painting are graceful and natural, resembling traces left behind by the vicissitudes of nature. The charm and allure of the beautiful color contrast are born from the painting's sense of motion. Lovely colors of pearl, emerald, agate, coral, aged jade, earthen yellow, beeswax, and giant clamshell join together in harmony. The effect of this painting can be easily summarized: This natural combination of colors brings about the enjoyment of aesthetic pleasure.

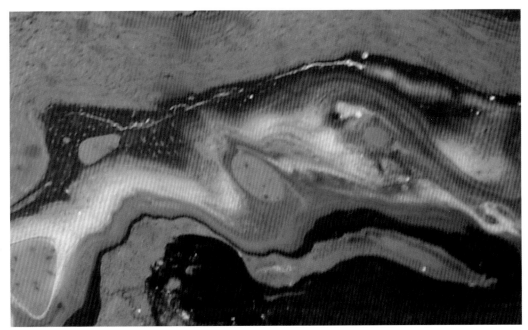

Ying She Dou
(The Eagle Vanquishes the Snake) (#50)

Artist: H.H. Dorje Chang Buddha III
Style: Kuangxi

"The Eagle Vanquishes the Snake" represents the truth that justice will eventually triumph over evil. The eagle represents justice and righteousness, and the snake is the symbol of terror and evil. The meaning expressed by this painting is that any evil act – no matter how savage and cruel, how deceitful and cunning, or how harmful to living beings – will in the end be defeated by justice and righteousness, represented by the mighty eagle. This painting displays the mighty, fierce, fearsome appearance of the eagle and its awe-inspiring, unstoppable sense of righteous honor.

The eagle and the snake were painted with fine, meticulous brushwork. On the other hand, the accompanying withered tree trunk was painted with bold, vigorous strokes of the free-hand style. It has the charm of a casual style together with the scholarly air and graceful ancient look typical of engraved stone seals. Unaffected, seasoned, extraordinary artistic skills are embodied in an image that simply lacks any sign of mediocrity. This remarkable work that very successfully depicts unyielding moral courage is in the "Kuangxi" style.

Zi Se Shan Zhuang
(Purple Mountain Villa) (#220)

Artist: H.H. Dorje Chang Buddha III

This painting is filled with purple. Such painting technique usually does not work because of the monotony of one color. However, this artwork called "Purple Mountain Villa" is quite amazing in that it radiates a type of intoxicating attraction. With careful observation, one will discover that such attractive force originates from a wondrous charm based on skillful brushwork rather than the coloring or layout of the painting. This is a result of the inner-attainment of an artist who not only truly understands the spirit of art, but who can adeptly depict the spirit of art. It is very telling that true art provides wonderful, mind-comforting enjoyment without the need to view any particular shape, image, or color.

Kong Kong Xiao Niu Zha
(Small Empty Cattle Pen) (#109) **(partial picture)**

Artist: H.H. Dorje Chang Buddha III
Style: Banqi

This work is painted in the "Banqi" style. This painting intriguingly possesses both the effect of being powerfully carved by a knife as well as the charm of watery ink brush strokes. The wooden pen, for example, composed of a small number of simple brush strokes, exhibits the vivid appeal of watery ink. The thatched huts unimaginatively arrayed inside the pen are depicted with the utmost simplicity and absence of artificiality.

This painting expresses a transcendent artistry by displaying the extraordinary within the ordinary. Although the painting does not depict cattle, the rich contents that fill its spaces lead the viewer to enjoy a sense of the presence of cattle despite their absence.

(#15)

Gu Cheng Yu Yi (#15)
(Ancient City in the Rain)

Artist: H.H. Dorje Chang Buddha III

The painting "Ancient City in the Rain" was created in Chengdu, China by H.H. Dorje Chang Buddha III in His youth. This work carries on an ancient style yet also contains innovation. It has a three-dimensional visual effect associated with western paintings. The artistic conception is to depict the modern look of an ancient city. The brush strokes convey an ancient style characteristic of magnanimity, and the added details convey boundless feelings. Spring rain is falling continuously at the break of dawn when the first rays of the sun emerge. Morning dew appears, nurtured by the morning wind and an air of vitality. Pedestrians wearing rain coats bustle about with open umbrellas. They rush about to make a living. Day after day, they go on like this until their lives end. This scene makes people sigh over the impermanence of life.

Xiao Xiong Mao
(Lesser Panda) (#210)
(partial picture)

Artist: H.H. Dorje Chang Buddha III

This reddish animal is very rare and precious. People call it the lesser panda. H.H. Dorje Chang Buddha III created this painting using freehand brushwork. The essence of the appeal of this painting lies with the coloring of the lesser panda. The natural-looking tail-rings and spots of the lesser panda convey an attractive sense of beauty. There is also the small drooping willow with its round leaves. It was made using a calligraphic method that is applied in Chinese paintings. That technique was applied in a very skillful and seasoned way.

Golden Lotuses (#78) (partial picture)

Artist: Yu Hua Shouzhi Wang

There is an ancient saying that the embellishment of one red dot in otherwise all green vegetation provides a noticeable elegant charm emotionally appealing in myriad ways. The meaning of that saying is that red flowers should be used to complement green leaves in order to depict the best setting. However, the approach of Yu Hua Shouzhi Wang to draw flowers in gold and create leaves with splashed watery ink exhibits even higher elegance, greater beauty, and lovelier simplicity. The technique of Yu Hua Shouzhi Wang to paint lotus flowers in varying degrees of darkness and lightness enables her to represent fully a striking charm in both tone and form.

Every stroke is lively, vigorous, graceful, and without the slightest air of affectation. Applying mature and seasoned artistry, she fully displays on paper her unfettered, natural, unattached state of mind. The brushwork was completed with ease and spontaneity, free of any inhibition. The atmosphere is strong but very elegant and pure. This entire painting provides much comfort to the eyes.

Xing Yuan Ri Li Shan (partial picture)
(Xing Garden at Mount Rili) (#103)

Artist: H.H. Dorje Chang Buddha III
Style: Miaoxie

Painted by the artist at Xing Garden in 1993, "Xing Garden at Mount Rili" portrays the natural world of steep cliffs. Vibrant green depicts moss and grass widely spread over rocks. This painting was later captured as a photograph and inscribed with the title "Xing Garden at Mount Rili." The original painting, however, was never inscribed. More than ten years later, the piece was refined and refinished, and interestingly, it was simply inscribed as "Mount Rili."

This painting adopts the techniques of the "Miaoxie" style of painting. When examining the brushwork carefully, you will discover interweaving brush strokes that resemble the crisscrossing of thin wires, creating change and variation as well as revealing a multitude of emotions and intrigue through their complexity. The excellence in technique is reflected in the spirit of the work, including the limitless appeal of the illusory watery ink.

When observed from near or far, the painting appears to depict the natural scene of a bottomless waterfall painted in fine, meticulous brushwork. If you carefully examine the subtle details of the painting's brushwork, however, you will be startled by the vigorous brush touches. There is substance within emptiness and order amid seeming chaos. An artistic beauty born of free, natural brush strokes infuses this painting. Through the strength and power of vigorous brush strokes, the artist unveils the extraordinary aesthetic charm lying within the simple scene of a waterfall between two cliffs.

Crane Dance (#72)

Artist: H.H. Dorje Chang Buddha III

"Crane Dance" refers to red-crowned cranes dancing. This work of calligraphy was written in 1990 in Sichuan, China. At that time, the government of China at the highest national level was building the one and only museum built by the government in honor of a living person.

It was named the "Museum of Master Wan Ko Yee." However, to people's surprise, H.H. Dorje Chang Buddha III went to the museum only three times all together after its construction was completed. He stated that it was not His museum, that it belonged to everyone, and that He could not use it for His own enjoyment.

Thus, He lifted His brush and wrote the two Chinese characters for "Crane Dance." He explained that red-crowned cranes tend not to build nests for themselves since they often stay in various places. When quiet, they frequently engage in meditational observation. When in motion, they frequently dance. Their nature is noble, pure, elegant and simple. They develop their virtue, are not attached to a specific abode, and take care of themselves so as to enjoy their natural lifespan. That is why since ancient times they have been praised for their longevity.

French River Landscape (#370)

Artist: Frits Thaulow (1847~1906)

Frits Thaulow was a Norwegian impressionist painter and engraver. Originally wanting to become a marine painter, he studied at the art academy in Copenhagen (1870-73) as well as with the Danish marine specialist C. F. Sørensen (1818-79). He also became an expert at painting slow-flowing rivers and complex reflections in water, particularly during his autumn and winter stay beside the Simoa River at Modum in 1883, when he produced such paintings as 'Winter at Simoa'.

During the 1880s he was prominent in establishing more progressive artists' associations and exhibition societies in Norway and was regarded as the leading Norwegian artist of the period. He decided to move to France in 1892, living at Camiers, Etaples and Montreuil as well as Paris (1892-1894, 1898-1906) and Dieppe (1894-1898). He painted about 50 pictures a year, most of them rather small. A large number of these pictures were river scenes of great virtuosity, but he also rendered poetic nocturnes, townscapes, harbor scenes, quaint bridges and even marines. Thaulow was essentially a painter working within the framework of Realism and Impressionism.

His works are collected by renowned museums throughout the world, including the Pinakothek in Munich, National Museum of Sweden in Stockholm, and museums in Berlin, Brussels, Copenhagen, Hamburg, Oslo, Paris, Strasbourg, Venice and many cities in the United States.

Depart de Bateaux de Peche, Ostende (#349)

Artist: Paul Hermanus (1859~1911)

Now regarded as one of the pre-eminent Belgian painters of the Nineteenth Century, Paul Hermanus was a Realist painter whose work possesses a Luminist quality. He was born in Brussels in 1859, the son of the painter Alexandre Hermanus, and as a young boy took his initial studies with his father. In 1870, at the age of only eleven, he enrolled at the Academy of Brussels to study oil painting. Around 1885 his career started in earnest, and he was soon garnering the attention of the critics who fell in love with his dramatic coastal scenes and town views. In 1899 he was commissioned to paint a series of frescoes for the Maison Communale d'Uccle that can still be seen today.

This highly important example of his work dates to 1903, considered his most important period. Entitled in French on the reverse as 'The Departure of the Fishing Boats, Ostend', Hermanus depicts a busy seascape with his customary skills. Of additional merit is the presence of the original gold leaf frame manufactured by the Brussels frame maker Philippe Cerusier, with the original label to the reverse.

Paul Hermanus died at the tragically young age of only fifty-one but left behind a body of work of great variety and consistency. His paintings are collected by many prominent museums in Belgium and other countries, including the Musee Des Beaux Arts, Brussels and the Museum Voor Moderne Kunst, Ostend.

Dong Fen (partial picture)
(Winter Powder) (#80)

Artist: H.H. Dorje Chang Buddha III

This plum blossom painting conveys a feeling of beauty and realism. The arrangement and structure of the branches, twigs and flowers prominently demonstrate the total proficiency of the artist in painting plum flowers, a proficiency that incorporates both ancient ways and novel ideas. Without this proficiency, it would be impossible to paint such lifelike flowers with such natural structures.

Bluish Plum Blossoms on Dancing Branches that Resemble Coiled Dragons (#81)

Artist: H.H. Dorje Chang Buddha III

This looks like the swirling and curling of soft ribbons. Then why does this painting so smoothly and gracefully exhibit vigorous and forceful brush strokes? And why does it so smoothly and gracefully exhibit a charm arising from the harmonious intermingling of dark and light hues? The answers lie in the artist's state of mind and command of brush and ink. The skills this painting reflects and the overall layout of this painting have their source in the uninhibited, casual, wildly free artistry of the artist. In painting and calligraphy, this is what is known as a natural state free of attachment. Firmness is contained within gentleness. Without having reached such a state, an artist would not dare apply this technique to paint dancing branches in the swirling-dragon style.

H.H. Dorje Chang Buddha III also composed a poem for this painting: "Dancing branches resembling coiled dragons declare their grace. Icy peaks at lofty heights, what need to fear the cold? This painting is totally devoid of the air of birth in this mundane world. I sigh that living beings have yet to see its face."

At the time of the New Year festival in winter, a most elegant and valued plum flower called "dong fen" (winter powder) will blossom. It is widely known to be the king of white plum blossoms. That is the subject of this painting by H.H. Dorje Chang Buddha III. A strong contrast is presented by the graceful dense ink that was used to paint the tree trunk and the whiting used to form the flowers. The spatial effect of farness adds to the charm of the picture, providing the viewer with an awareness of both emptiness and form. A very special aspect of this painting is that the artist did not apply powerful, bold strokes of uneven contour and content. Rather, ink was applied through a gradual moistening process, manifesting the strong talent of the artist. This is extremely rare.

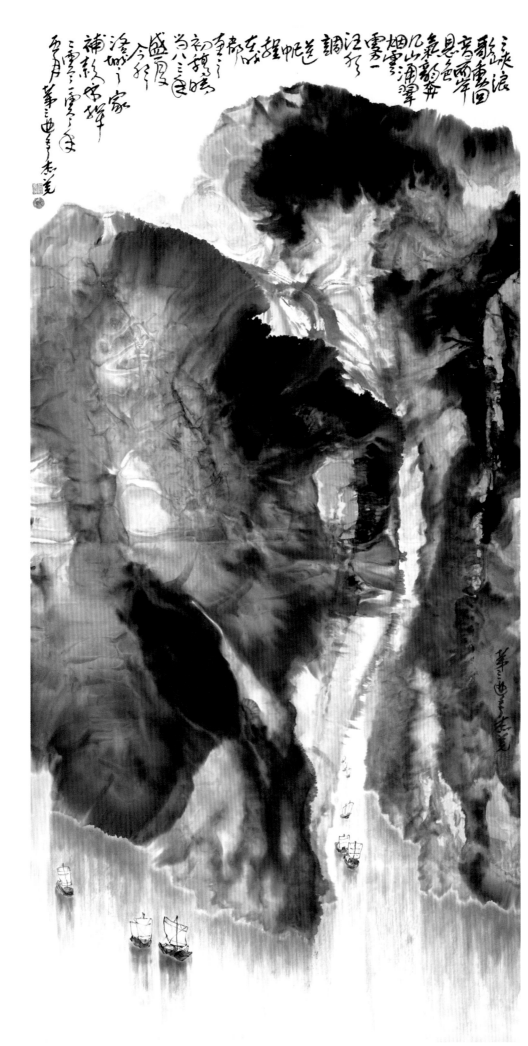

(#70)

74

San Xia Lang Ge
(Song of the Waves in the Three Gorges) (#70)
Artist: H.H. Dorje Chang Buddha III   Style: Pomo Weiyun

The style of "Song of the Waves in the Three Gorges" is typical of the "Pomo Weiyun" style of painting. This painting prominently features the grandeur of splash-ink coupled with the charm of water and ink colors. Its tone is heavy. The brushwork conveys a sense of powerful momentum, lively charm, and vividness similar to a scene on the ground after a long, moving river has just rolled by. The few small sailboats add to the elegance of this water scene as they cut through the water. The allure of the mighty river and awe-inspiring mountains with misty holy places cleanses one of all negative emotions. This painting indeed has a quality suggestive of poetry and calligraphy.

H.H. Dorje Chang Buddha III inscribed this painting with an elegant Chinese poem that translates as follows: "The song of waves echo in the gorge. Hanging colors of the two rocky cliffs burst with charm. Blue emerges from a few cloudy, misty mountains. The melody of vast water sends the sails on their way." This poem aptly describes the beautiful, misty landscape of the Three Gorges, where water and sky blend in harmony and human emotions are embedded in the scenery. This painting is an artistic paragon exemplifying poetic, calligraphic, and painting skills.

Wo Lai Ye (I Am Approaching) (#40)
(partial picture)

Artist: H.H. Dorje Chang Buddha III
Style: Kuangxi

H.H. Dorje Chang Buddha III created the first version of this painting when He was a child. It was later meticulously made into a quality work of art. On His ninth birthday, H.H. Dorje Chang Buddha III said, "I am nine years old today. I will take this opportunity of turning exactly nine years old to give an analogy. There exists holy dharma that is beyond the peak of the stages of the nine vehicles. As the saying goes, a Tathagata teaches dharma and in so doing is akin to a roaring lion. I come to this world to benefit living beings. This is my painting." The first version of this painting of a mighty lion entitled "I Am Approaching" was created by Wan Ko Yee when He was a nine-year-old child. However, He was not able to successfully complete it at that time. In recent years, H.H. Dorje Chang Buddha III again wielded His brush and completed this work using the technique characterized by the "Kuangxi" style of painting. This painting is truly an amazing feat of artistry. Regardless of where and at what angle you stand to view this painting, the mighty lion will always be looking at you and appear to be walking towards you. No matter how you change your viewing position, it will always move in response to your movements. This is truly a magical painting.

     Tacit Understanding Expressed
Through a Soft Smile (#67)

Artist: H.H. Dorje Chang Buddha III

This work is in the typical "child-mind" calligraphic style created by H.H. Dorje Chang Buddha III. It entails going back to simplicity and returning to naturalness. The brushwork contains a type of unsophisticated power. This work of calligraphy appears quite simple at first glance but is actually extremely difficult to write and evidences an extraordinarily high degree of calligraphic proficiency. It is an inscription written for a miraculous Yun sculpture and names that Yun sculpture. Its meaning is that tacit understanding is expressed through a soft smile. One must ponder deeply to realize its subtle message.

濟公活佛

(#31)

76

Ji Gong Huo Fo
(Monk Jigong) (#31)

Artist: H.H. Dorje Chang Buddha III

"Monk Jigong" is a figure in Buddhism, a holy Arhat known to almost everyone in China. He applied his vast supernatural powers to benefit the public. Through his boundless dharma powers, he helped and saved people, punished evil, and promoted goodness. In China, there have been many movies, television productions, and writings in which he is highly praised. With the wondrous touch of his brush, the artist applied the fine brushwork technique to realistically reveal details of the skin, meridians, and veins of Monk Jigong. Combining these two elements of fine brushwork and realism, the artist vividly portrayed the image of this figure who lived as a beggar in his daily life. Monk Jigong outwardly appeared to be an ugly, drunken man, a crazy beggar in ragged clothes. However, hidden deep in his heart was a determination to benefit living beings out of great compassion. All day long he constantly helped people, feeling it was his duty to provide others with happiness.

Yi Chen Bu Ran (Immaculate) (#207)

Artist: H.H. Dorje Chang Buddha III
Style: Fanpu

With only a small number of strokes, a comforting and natural appeal appears vividly on paper. The style is neither overly cautious nor affected. A scholarly tone and an air of stone seals are revealed in the brushwork. This is a work of art with an attractiveness that stems from mature skills. The title "Immaculate" means that this painting is free of any trace of the mundane. It is in the "Fanpu" style.

Great Accomplishment Is Attained Only Through Selflessness (#35)

Artist: H.H. Dorje Chang Buddha III

This work of calligraphy is in the steel brush-tip technique. There is a striking steely, powerful calligraphic style to this work entitled "Great Accomplishment Is Attained Only Through Selflessness." It conveys a sense of utmost firmness, like that of iron or steel.

There is profound meaning to the sentence "Great accomplishment is attained only through selflessness." As human beings living in this world, we must first let go of "self." Day and night we should stay far away from selfishness and should derive our happiness from benefiting others. When attachment to the concept of self is absent in our thoughts, we become free of selfishness and greed. Our minds become bright, clear, and free of impediments. We then consider the interests of others and are naturally respected by others. Consequently, we are physically and mentally at ease and are happy. Through this natural process, one can successfully refine one's state of mind to be broad, elevated, and pure until one eventually attains the complete elimination of all defilements.

Unique Lotuses in Ink (#63)
(partial picture)

Artist: Yu Hua Shouzhi Wang

This painting's arrangement is classically simple and straightforward. The brushwork conveys both simplicity and adeptness. Each lotus stem was painted with just one stroke from top to bottom. The important fact is that the artist dared to adopt an extremely plain and uncreative artistic conception, yet remarkably powerful, seasoned painting skills casually applied are reflected deep within this painting. This work also reveals the artist's inner power based on her broadmindedness. Even more wonderful is the fact that no touchups whatsoever were added to the lotus stems to enhance their charm. Painting skills alone were relied upon to capture both the spirit and form of the stems, resulting in a very genuine-looking image. The seedpod, flower, and leaves are in complete concert with one another. The style is vivacious, elegant, free of conventionality, and wonderfully spellbinding.

Anyone who does not believe in the difficulty of painting a lotus stem with just one stroke can try it himself. He will then know how very difficult it is. A work of this quality can only be successfully created by an artist who has reached great heights in painting and whose artistry is devoid of any trace of vulgarity. This is a precious painting in which the extraordinary can be seen within the seemingly ordinary. It is no wonder that Yu Hua Shouzhi Wang was praised by experts as "the unmatched master of lotus flower paintings from ancient times to now" when her artwork was exhibited in the United States Capitol.

Lions, created in 2010 (#260)
(partial picture)

Artist: Guo Ruyu   Style: Abstract painting

Professor Guo Ruyu was born in China in December of 1941. He is a member of the Artists Association of China. His positions include Director of the Creation and Research Department of the Sichuan Province Poetry, Calligraphy and Painting Institute; President of the Chengdu City Fine Brushwork Painting Association; Dean of Chengdu Fine Brushwork Painting Academy; and Dean of Sichuan Province Oriental Painting Art Academy.

The subject of this painting called "Lions" is a group of lions who have just begun to awaken. It expresses the awakening of lions. The lion is the king of all beasts and the symbol of strength. The artist uses the theme of a group of awakened lions that have various expressions--some of the lions roar in anger, some have looks of disdain, and some show great resentment.

The artist used rough and bold brushwork to provide a sense of strength and enhance the motif of restlessness featured in this painting. A large amount of red was used in the painting. Modern artistic techniques were applied to depict lions with different appearances and dispositions. There are ample variations in the appearances of the lions.

This painting harmoniously blends techniques from Chinese and Western painting into one whole. Its colors are strong, as is its impact on the viewer. It is rich in creativity, and the underlying artistic conception is novel. This painting combines both Chinese and Western artistry.

Quay Scene with Figures & Boats (#360)

Artist: Rafael Joseffy (1852~1915)

Although much better remembered as a musician, Rafael Joseffy was also a talented artist, as this beautiful seascape would attest. Painted in 1882, it is inscribed with the word 'Wien,' which is the Austrian form of the city Vienna. Paintings by Rafael Joseffy are extremely rare and although it is unclear as to where he was trained as an artist, it is assumed that he just possessed an extraordinary natural talent for painting. Most of the paintings that survive are painted in oils, although a few drawings and watercolors also are known.

From the paintings that we can identify as his work, we see that he attempted a number of differing subject matters. In the 1990's a painting by Joseffy appeared at a public sale in Austria. That work depicted an extensive mountain scene in the Austrian Alps and was painted with the same exactitude as this example. In the 1970's another work surfaced, that being a lake scene, probably also in the Alpine region. That painting was of the identical size as this example.

This particular work by Joseffy is one of his extremely hard to come by works of art.

Lotuses (#264)

Artist: Guo Ruyu   Style: Chinese Fine Brushwork Painting

Lotuses appear very often in Oriental paintings. This depiction belongs to the realm of fine brushwork painting. The artist painted it applying watery ink of a single-color. The birds and flowers were depicted with somewhat light coloring to enhance their visual quality and emphasize the motif. This is a very special way of treating the scene, resulting in an interesting and charming portrayal. This work of art reflects the personal style of the artist in fine brushwork painting.

Lao Nong Shai Gu Chang
(An Old Farmer's Grain-Drying Yard) (#218)

Artist: H.H. Dorje Chang Buddha III
Style: Xiangtong

This simple, bright, and lively image was completed with casual application of the brush and no mental attachment on the part of the artist. That is how this naturally appealing artwork in the "Xiangtong" style came into being. The scene is an empty grain-drying yard. The farmhouses and the densely black trees form a delightful contrast. The mountains are not like real mountains, and the trees do not resemble real trees. The mountains and trees harmoniously fuse into one integral whole, presenting a subtly appealing scene.

What underlies all of this? It is the artist's ability to create an enchanting image in which one does not see precisely painted objects, yet one nonetheless feels aesthetic pleasure over seeing such a natural atmosphere. This amazing and unusual phenomenon is the spirit or soul of art.

Portrait of an Officer (#366)

Artist: David Martin (1737~1797)

David Martin was a leading Scottish painter of portraits, and he was born in Anstruther on April 1st 1737. Martin painted over 300 portraits in his lifetime. One of the earliest independent ones is the 1767 one of Benjamin Franklin (now in the White House, Washington, DC). His most influential works depict Scottish Enlightenment figures like the chemist Joseph Black (1787) and the philosopher David Hume (1770), and noblewomen such as the Honorable Barbara Gray (1787). In 1785 he was appointed principal painter to the Prince of Wales in Scotland.

The officer depicted in this painting is seen wearing the uniform of the Sixth (or Inniskilling) Regiment of Dragoons; an extremely likely candidate would be William, Lord Banff, who had joined the regiment on May 2nd 1780 and had, by 1789, attained the rank of Captain. Dr. Allan Carsewell of the Department of Armed Forces History, part of the National Museums of Scotland, has provided the information above.

Works by David Martin are collected by internationally famed museums, including the National Portrait Gallery, the H.M. Queen Elizabeth Collection in London, and other museums in Scotland, Australia and the United States.

Jade Panel Painted in Oil Colors - Emerald Jade (#308)

Artist: H.H. Dorje Chang Buddha III   Style: Chaoshi

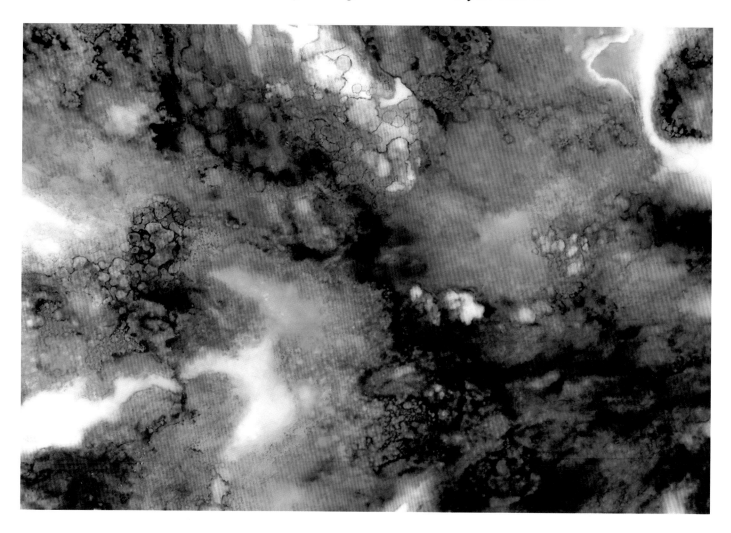

A poem composed by H.H. Dorje Chang Buddha III, which has five characters to each line, translates as follows: "Green jade of watery tone; what a treasure among majestic gemstones. Not stored even in celestial mountains; painting skills opened the wonderful door to it." This poem lifts the veil covering the features of this striking emerald green faux jade that has a watery tone. It is as if it had just emerged from the bottom of a heavenly lake. Water seems to linger on its surface and permeate deeply, layer by layer. With refracting, penetrating sunlight, this jadeite is even more heartwarming.

Real jadeite like this in the size of only the mouth of a bowl would be as precious as the Jade of He (probably the most famous piece of jade in Chinese history, unearthed more than 2,700 years ago). However, this emerald jade before you was created by H.H. Dorje Chang Buddha III using the "Chaoshi" style of painting. It is a gigantic piece that cannot be found on earth. That is exactly why it can be described as "a treasure among majestic gemstones." Its largeness is unparalleled in the world, and its majestic, elegant, imposing air is unprecedented.

"Celestial mountains" refers to the mountains of the gods in heaven. The verse "not stored even in celestial mountains" means that even if the gods in heaven wanted to acquire such precious jade made from painting, their wish would not be fulfilled. The fact is that this precious jade is not stored in the mountains of the gods in heaven.

We now know that this rectangular faux gemstone is not from the celestial world. Rather, it was created by H.H. Dorje Chang Buddha III through brushwork and color application. This vivid and fresh faux jadeite is based on natural jadeite but excels the beauty that nature can provide. It is bright, gorgeous, and genuine-looking, and is in the category of glass-like jade.

Dutch River Landscape with Figures (#355)

Artist: Charles Henri Joseph Leickert (1816~1907)

Charles Henri Joseph Leickert was born on September 22, 1816 in Brussels. Leickert began his artistic training at the age of eleven. In 1827, his father enrolled him in The Hague Drawing Academy, where he studied under Bartholomeus van Hove (1790- 1880), the well-known artist of landscapes and cityscapes. Around 1835 Leickert joined the studio of Wijnand Nuyen (1813-1839), the painter who specialized in landscape paintings. Nuyen's tutelage is evident in his choice of picturesque townscapes with lively details, such as laundry and pigeons.

Leickert's next and most influential teacher was Andreas Schelfhout (1787-1870), the renowned artist best known for his winter scenes. It was under Schelfhout that Leickert diligently learned to paint winter scenes, and he rapidly absorbed his master's working methods. In 1856, Leickert joined the Board of Governors of the Royal Academy of Fine Art in Amsterdam. The years following his arrival in Amsterdam until the 1870s were Leickert's most successful. During that period, he produced a wider variety of themes that included more beach and dune scenes.

His works are collected by a number of world-renowned museums, including the Rijksmuseum in Amsterdam, Netherlands and the Hermitage in St. Petersburg, Russia.

Ji Jiao Shan Zhong
(Amid Chicken-Foot Mountain) (#274)

Artist: H.H. Dorje Chang Buddha III

This work is a real-life portrayal by H.H. Dorje Chang Buddha III in His earlier years and was created when He visited Chicken-Foot Mountain at the end of autumn. While standing on one mountain, the artist captured the actual scene of the mountain across the valley. The layout is simple and concise. Emphasis is placed on the charm and appeal that exudes from the adroitly applied brush strokes and ink. The artist's mastery of calligraphy and painting and his ability to create natural-looking art free of mediocrity can be observed through the skillful techniques by which this painting was created.

Zui Zai Lu Se Hua Yuan (partial picture)
(Intoxicated in a Turquoise Garden) (#65)

Artist: H.H. Dorje Chang Buddha III

The brushwork of this painting is bold, vigorous, and completely unconstrained. Large, dancing strokes of a casual hand and free mind bring to form branches and twigs. Crisscrossing strokes may appear chaotic but in fact are not. The turquoise plum blossom is a rare species of plum blossoms. These elegant, sublime flowers have a strong resistance to coldness and a scent that is quite fresh and fragrant. This painting has a vigorous and firm style yet maintains great simplicity. Observe the vivid appeal of watery ink. Its special characteristic is rigorous structure even though the splash-ink technique was used. The transitions of the brushwork display a quality born of charm. The vivid appeal of watery ink can even be seen in the details of this painting.

Emerald Jade (#76)
Artist: H.H. Dorje Chang Buddha III

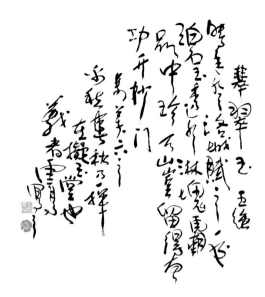

Each of the rapid cursive writing styles of famous Chinese calligraphers throughout history has its own merits. Additionally, numerous varieties of calligraphy have evolved from the different forms of Chinese characters, such as the regular script, cursive script, official script, and seal character. The most famous calligraphers in the rapid cursive style are Wang Xizhi, Zhang Huaiguan, and He Shaoji. One of the foremost calligraphers of modern times is Master Youren Yu. However, H.H. Dorje Chang Buddha III is totally different from all other great masters of calligraphy. It can be said that He created more calligraphic styles than any other calligrapher in the world, including calligraphers throughout the history of Chinese calligraphy. H.H. Dorje Chang Buddha III has written calligraphy in forms and styles that He Himself created, such as the childlike form, the dragon and snake form, the semi-cursive script, the small cursive script, the large cursive script, the jade belt script, and the steel bone script. He has developed many calligraphic styles that reflect the quintessence of calligraphic charm.

This high quality work in the rapid cursive style reflects great calligraphic abilities. It is devoid of the constraints of ancient styles that others have rigidly adhered to and is free of the limitations inherent in rubbings from stone inscriptions. Created with an unfettered hand and unattached mind, it has the appearance of a celestial writing accomplished with a childlike mind and steady strokes of the brush. It is naturally attractive and reflects complete calligraphic proficiency. No trace of the mundane can be found. It is a work that exemplifies appealing gracefulness, flowing charm, and brisk elegance.

Xi Zhen Yi Shou (Rare Exotic Animals) (#265)

Artist: H.H. Dorje Chang Buddha III
Style: Kuangxi

This work of art is in the "Kuangxi" style of painting. Pandas are one of the most common subjects in Chinese paintings of animals. Because a panda is a precious and rare animal, it is the emblem of the World Society for the Protection of Animals. All over the world, there are countless paintings of pandas. However, most of them have a stilted, mediocre style. Why? It is because such paintings lack a suitable overall layout and matching surrounding scene. This is not merely a matter of technique. The fundamental reason lies with the artist's lack of knowledge. Consequently, the artist's inner temperament permeates through the brush tip onto the paper, exhibiting an overall sense of conventional, common artistry. Such an artist depicts only the superficial appearance of the subject and is unable to reveal the intrinsic spirit and charm of the subject.

As an example, every literate Chinese person knows how to write the Chinese characters that mean you, I (me), and he (him). The strokes one must complete to write such characters are the same for everyone. However, these same three characters will have two totally different levels of quality depending upon whether they were written by those with calligraphic skills or those without calligraphic skills. What is the cause that differentiates good quality characters from bad quality characters? It is the inner-charm or attractiveness of the characters.

The same is true in painting. Suppose two people apply a single downward stroke of the brush. One stroke looks as dead and stiff as a corpse. The other stroke looks totally alive and delicate. The key difference is whether a spirit or life-force in embodied within that stroke. Additionally, if an artist wants to attain a certain high level of applying powder (i.e. applying white) in his Chinese paintings, he must be able to convey a clear sense of cleanliness. Particularly in ink-and-wash paintings of pandas, the lifelike, charming and naturally varying white fur of the pandas must be prominently featured. However, artists frequently produce a sense of dirtiness when they use both ink and powder. There is an overall air of griminess enveloping the painting.

In contrast, panda paintings by H.H. Dorje Chang Buddha III are completely different. They look as if they were created by a magical heavenly brush. There is an extremely vivacious appeal, a deeply touching liveliness to these pandas. Pervading such paintings is an air of purity, cleanliness, and hopefulness.

The three pandas in this painting all have innocent expressions and look vividly real. The scattered perspective technique of Chinese paintings was combined with the three-dimensional perspective technique of oil paintings. The colors are richly charming, and the layout is exquisite. Empty space and color are mutually complimentary in a fascinating way. The pandas and the surrounding scene blend into one harmonious image. These lifelike pandas painted in fine brushwork with meticulous attention to detail contrast perfectly with the surrounding scene painted in freehand brushwork. The painting style is plain, vigorous and mature. There is order within the seeming disorder and interesting juxtaposition between the real and the abstract. The achievement of using complimentary bold and delicate strokes in one painting, as H.H. Dorje Chang Buddha III does, sets His artistry apart from conventional artistry.

Beyond Craftsmanship (#278)

Artist: H.H. Dorje Chang Buddha III
Style: Weiyin

In the art of painting, the most important factors are the interactions among colors and the arrangement of space and substance. Artists use colors to reveal space, and space to bring out colors. The colors used should not be showy or inelegant. As for the emotional sentiments that a painting conveys, it seems that perspectives vary from one person to the next. Everyone, however, is able to determine for himself whether a painting evokes feelings of comfort and happiness or irritability and repulsion.

"Beyond Craftsmanship," which belongs to the "Weiyin" style of painting is the kind of work that engenders feelings of aesthetic pleasure. More outstandingly, this painting could be divided into a few dozen individual pieces that, when enlarged, are all works of art on their own in the "Weiyin" style.

鷄場于之二三汲月三九一毛車在者

大師弥畫雲庭高義

鎗璧之墨

全年時成都於雲高

(#19)

Ji Chang Yi Jiao
(Part of a Chicken Farm)
(#19)

Artist: H.H. Dorje Chang Buddha III

A simple and ordinary chicken farm in the countryside seems to have been drawn from casual movement of the brush. Actually, this painting exhibits elegance, a harmonious overall arrangement, and adept, unadorned artistry. Where the image is real, it is not stilted. Where the image is surreal, it is not chaotic. An agile yet rigorous approach was used. The coloring is plain but attractive. This painting markedly manifests the style of merging calligraphy and painting into one whole. One will be even more impressed when viewing this painting carefully. This work of art was written rather than painted. Only by attaining very high calligraphic skills and artistic accomplishment can one apply the center brush-tip technique to draw such lines. This painting is full of life and contains within it the talent and learning of the artist. This one sheet of paper with its ink brush strokes seems to encompass heaven, earth, and nature.

Lao Hu (Tiger) (#45)

Artist: H.H. Dorje Chang Buddha III
Style: Fangfa

This grey tiger was painted in the "Fangfa" style. Such painting technique was created for the first time in this human world by H.H. Dorje Chang Buddha III, and He is the only one who possesses it. No professional painter can replicate it with his own brushwork. Anyone will understand this truth by just trying to do so. This painting depicts a gray tiger climbing a mountain. The tiger has an awe-inspiring appearance, a valiant and majestic bearing. Its two front paws are as big as tortoise shells, and its two fangs look like a steel fork. Wind follows it as it walks along a path. While sitting on the ground, it looks over the distant mountain valley. Upon climbing to the top, it assumes a heroic, imposing posture. It turns its head and all other beasts flee in fear.

H.H. Dorje Chang Buddha III has decided not to make this type of painting anymore. Therefore, existing paintings in the "Fangfa" style have become rare treasures. The inscription on this painting is "Dorje Chang III." It is also stamped with the three-dimensional, eight-jewel, gold-inlaid fingerprint seal. That makes it an even more precious and rare work of art.

Mao (Cat) (#43)

Artist: H.H. Dorje Chang Buddha III
Style: Fangfa

This painting named "Cat" is in the "Fangfa" style. Magical appeal underlies this painting. This creative technique comes from a state of wisdom. That is why it not an ordinary painting. The accompanying scene near the cat was painted with only a small number of brush strokes yet contains the style of stone seals and an air of scholarship. Although ink was used in a sparing way, the form and spirit of the scene are captured.

H.H. Dorje Chang Buddha III has decided not to make this type of magically charming painting anymore. He has not since created another work of the same type of unsurpassed artistry. Thus, this painting is a form of art that has been discontinued.

Reclining Nude in a Landscape (#363)

Artist: Jean-Jacques Henner (1829~1905)

The sixth and last child of Alsatian peasants, Jean-Jacques Henner became an extremely successful portraitist and painter of female nudes in Second Empire and Third Republic Paris. His oeuvre included religious pictures, landscapes, and still-lifes as well.

The most significant influences on Henner's popular female nudes were the works of Correggio and those by the French artist Prud'hon. Debuting at the Salon of 1863 with 'Young Bather Asleep' (1862, Musee Unterlinden, Colmar) and two portraits, Henner won a third-class medal. He exhibited regularly for the next forty years and eventually won almost every award then available to artists. Henner painted his famous nudes with broad heavy strokes and used sfumato to soften their contours. Endowed with milky flesh and russet hair, they were consistently set against shadowy brown-toned landscapes.

In 1903, two years before his death, Henner was named Grand Officer of the Legion of Honor. Works by Jean-Jacques Henner are collected by the Louvre, the Musee de Jean-Jacques Henner in Paris and by many museums in France, Sweden, Russia and Canada.

Old Temple in Spring in Which No One Is Seen (#230)

Artist: H.H. Dorje Chang Buddha III
Style: Banqi

Red walls and black roof tiles appear indistinctly, partially hidden by the forest. It seems that no one comes to visit this old temple made up of several buildings. What kind of place is this? This is a holy place with celestial grass of jade-like beauty and a heavenly ancient monastery.

When inscribing this painting, the artist named it, "An old temple in spring in which no one is seen. A monk here attained the enlightened mind of Zen long ago." The meaning of this is extremely profound and broad. Its message is that this is the residence of a superior person, a monk who is a master. That master long ago attained enlightenment and entered the meditative state of emptiness and joy. That is why ordinary people are unable to see his physical body.

Deeply embedded within this painting is a simple yet riveting artistic force. This artwork combines the style of stone seal engravings and a scholarly air. It has the charm of a painting by the Western master of art, Van Gogh, but it also embodies learning and talent characteristic of Eastern culture. It is an idyllic scene of subtle beauty.

Ji Chang (Chicken Farm) (#217)

Artist: H.H. Dorje Chang Buddha III
Style: Fanpu

This painting engenders a naturally satisfying feeling. The style is uninhibited and bold. The lines and brush touches are flowing and smooth, without the slightest affectation. The application of brush and ink conveys a very strong sense that this artist is a great master with profound and extensive knowledge, not just a person specializing in painting alone. Otherwise, it would be impossible for this painting to possess such a scholarly air and embody such consummate artistry.

This artwork is in the "Fanpu" style.

The Old Mill at Heule – Nighttime (#368)

Artist: Emmanuel Vierin (1869~1954)

Born in Kortrijk on June 30, 1869, Vierin was a pupil at the Kortrijk Academy and at the Higher Institute for Fine Arts in Antwerp under Coosemans. Much of his subsequent life was spent in academia, with his nomination as teacher at the Academy of Kortrijk in 1896 and directorship in 1912.

His paintings have a poetic quality and are related to impressionism. Much of his work depicted landscape views in and around Antwerp and Bruges. He was particularly interested in the play of light within his subjects, a talent clearly evident in this example.

This important painting of the artist's work, previously in the collection of the family of the painter, dates to around 1901, considered Vierin's finest period. It depicts the old water-mill in the village of Heule, near Kortrijk, a view Vierin painted on a number of occasions. In fact, one of his famous paintings currently housed at the Museum of Fine Arts in Antwerp depicts this water-mill, although that work shows it during the summer months. His paintings are collected by important museums, including the Palais Des Beaux Arts in Brussels, Belgium and the National Art Museum of Catalonia in Barcelona, Spain.

Jade Panel Painted in Oil Colors - Good-Fortune and Longevity Jade
(#311)

Artist: H.H. Dorje Chang Buddha III   Style: Chaoshi

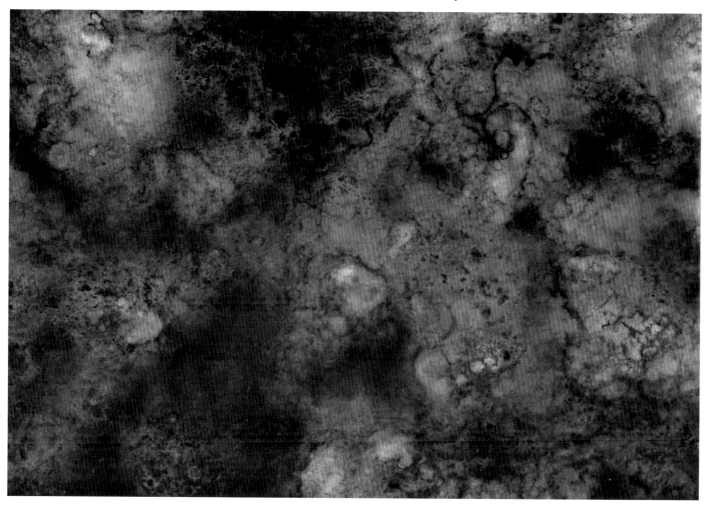

H.H. Dorje Chang Buddha III wrote a poem for "Good-Fortune and Longevity Jade" that translates as, "Good-fortune and longevity are extended to match the heavenly realm; green tinged with red presents profound charm of colors. A stone from a pedestal floating like a cloud in the third-level of the Tusita Heaven; I spontaneously smile without shame."

The meaning is that this colossal and extraordinarily beautiful jade of good-fortune and longevity did not come into being in the land or waters of the human realm. Rather, its inspiration came from the Tusita Heaven of celestial beings. This pedestal of the gods floating among the clouds contains the beautiful wish of blessings and extended longevity.

The dark green is steady and deep. There is the charm of splash-ink found in an ink-and-wash painting. The image is concentrated but not stiff, reflecting a broad mindset that is both poised and dynamic. Several salient red and light emerald green spots illuminate the jade's color scheme, like instantly intoxicating smiles in a very sedate setting. This extraordinarily beautiful jade of good-fortune and longevity that can only be found in the celestial world was painted using "Chaoshi" style techniques. It is a real artistic treat brought to this human world through the brushwork of H.H. Dorje Chang Buddha III.

Xiong Shi (Powerful Gaze)
(#42)

Artist: H.H. Dorje Chang Buddha III
Style: Fangfa

This work belonging to the "Fangfa" style of painting exemplifies a style of art where the extraordinary is seen within the ordinary. The technique and artistic conception it embodies are very subtle and profound. This painting called "Powerful Gaze" represents magnanimous, courageous, extraordinary sentiments. Wonders are seen within that which is ordinary.

Still-Life with Fruit & Nuts on a Ledge (#354)

Artist: Edward Ladell (1821~1886)

Edward Ladell's obituary in The Essex County Standard considered him "the foremost man of his day in fruit painting." He was entirely self-taught. He exhibited at the Royal Academy between 1856 and 1886, and also at the British Institute, the Royal Society of British Artists, Suffolk Street and local West Country venues. Ladell became immensely successful and the finest English still-life painter of his generation.

Ladell specialized in still-lifes composed of fruit, flowers and a variety of objects, including glass, tankards, china vases and bird's nests. His technique achieved an astonishing degree of realism. The works of Ladell are collected by many museums in Europe, including the Royal Albert Memorial Museum in Essex and the Harrogate City Art Gallery.

Tao Hua Shan Zhuang Qing Huai Hu (#27) (Lake of Feelings in Peach Blossom Mountain Village) (partial picture)

Artist: H.H. Dorje Chang Buddha III
Style: Pomo Xiantiao Xiezhen

This painting depicts a portion of "Lake of Feelings in Peach Blossom Mountain Village" near the banks of the Qinghuai River. It seems like a place where immortals go, with its green mountains and water, white cliffs, valleys of pines, floating clouds and mist, green paths decorated with maples and flowers, and beautiful houses.

It is a scenic spot whose beauty is unique in the entire world. It is said that this scenery resembles the view seen by someone who accidentally entered the Peach Garden Shangri-la. The brushwork of this painting is extraordinary, traditional, refined, and graceful and reveals a rather scholarly air. This artwork is characterized by the application of the center brush-tip technique coherently combined with the charm of the splash-ink technique plus details added through large-scale freehand brushwork. The different styles or techniques may appear separate from one another but actually intermingle, creating a scene with leisurely floating clouds and mist. This painting is done in the "Pomo Xiantiao Xiezhen" style.

Xue Hou Li Yuan (Pear Orchard After the Snow) (#222)

Artist: H.H. Dorje Chang Buddha III
Style: Banqi

This portrayal of a fruit orchard was created through a plain style of brushwork. The visual effect is an orchard after the melting of snow in midwinter. It was created through a most rigid painting method, yet it is natural-looking. This is due to technique and the artist's attainment in painting and calligraphy. It is a matter of the artist's brushwork skills.

Similar examples are the paintings of sunflowers by Van Gogh. Their arrangement is very plain and simple, yet they provide viewers with comfort and happiness. The key is the artistic effect produced from seasoned and skillful application of brush and colors. Paintings by H.H. Dorje Chang Buddha III embody this type of appeal born from mastery that transcends conventional painting techniques.

Hei Bai Xiong Zi (#87)
(Valliant Appearance) (partial picture)
Artist: H.H. Dorje Chang Buddha III
Style: Kuangxi

What you see here is a work named "Valliant Appearance" completed by the artist in His youth. A pair of vultures stands upright in a majestic pose on a fir tree. They look so lifelike, natural, proud, and imposing. Created by H.H. Dorje Chang Buddha III in 1980, this is one of the paintings that successfully represent the early stage of the "Kuangxi" style of painting that He pioneered. The vultures were realistically painted using fine brushwork and appear so very true to life and natural. The look of the fir leaves reveals that it is the end of autumn with winter fast approaching. Such precise, delicate, lifelike colors and brushwork are truly marvelous. In contrast, the tree trunk was painted in bold strokes through the large-scale freehand brushwork technique. The wonder of this painting lies with the harmony of boldness and precision, both of which together convey a single theme.

Even from the perspective of today, this painting is still an excellent work free of any trace of the mundane. The techniques, brushwork, application of ink and color, arrangement, conception, and overall quality pioneered the way for the founding of the "Kuangxi" style. Thus, H.H. Dorje Chang Buddha III lifted His brush, added an inscription on the right side of this painting, and stamped it with His three-dimensional, eight-jewel, gold-inlaid fingerprint seal.

Po Mo Pang Xie (Splash-Ink Crabs) (#34)
Artist: H.H. Dorje Chang Buddha III

"Splash-Ink Crabs" is a work from the artist's early years. It is well-known throughout calligraphy and painting circles that there have been numerous famous artists who painted crabs through the ink-and-wash technique. However, there has not been a single person who painted crabs through the splash-ink technique. This crab painting that you see today was accomplished through a painting method unprecedented in history. It realistically portrays the form of the crabs yet still maintains the natural grace that springs from splash-ink painting. Splash-ink charm on a minute scale can be seen from the tips of every angle of every leg.

Se Yun Tong Fei
(Color and Charm Fly Together) (#270)
Artist: H.H. Dorje Chang Buddha III
Style: Banqi

"Color and Charm Fly Together" means a special kind of appeal produced from the harmonious mixture of colors, watery ink, and space. This painting adheres to artistic tradition but also blazes new trails. It contains a rhythm only a person of learning could create and also evidences innovative, elegant artistry. Unadorned brush touches manifest the qualities of simplicity and steady maturity. No superficial gaudiness can be found.

This work has a scholarly atmosphere and a tone of engraved stone seals. Dark hues, light hues, realism, surrealism, and the charm of sculpting are intermingled in one cohesive whole. This painting belongs to the "Banqi" style.

Xi Wan Dan Qing Wu Ta Shi,
Xin Shou Pao Hao Jing Bu Qian
(I Casually Paint Simply for My Amusement
Without any Attachment) (#201)

Artist: H.H. Dorje Chang Buddha III
Style: Xiangtong and Banqi

What kind of painting is this that only uses three colors? The layout is simple. The trees and houses appear both real and abstract. What seems to be chaotic is not in disorder, for there is order amid the seeming chaos. The composition of this painting has the effect of one coherent whole. The two fishing boats look so rough, clumsy, yet sturdy. When viewing the entire scene, one can sense a quality of vigor that pervades everything. The brushwork is steady, reflects solid skills, and charm is deeply embedded within it.

If the viewer does not pay close attention, it will be difficult for him to discover that the skills underlying this brushwork are similar to those underlying the engraving of sharp edges. Thus, the painting has a particularly strong, natural flavor of engraved stone seals. However, the artistic conception and brush touches are also so innocent and childlike. This is a work of art with natural charm created through the artist's ability to return to the mindset of a child. This artwork is a combination of the "Xiangtong" and the "Banqi" styles of painting.

Za Chai Shi Gu (Brushwork Resembling Smashed Jade) (#211)

Artist: H.H. Dorje Chang Buddha III
Style: Fangfa

You can see that this nearly monotone painting completed with just a small number of strokes actually has the sturdy appeal of stone seal engravings. There is a phrase used in commenting upon Chinese paintings and calligraphy that relates to smashed jade. This painting exemplifies that charming style of smashed jade.

It is said that the key to a high-quality painting is that it contain the brush touches of calligraphy, the powerful air of engraved stone seals, a tone that comes from the artist's mastery of literature, a style that stems from the artist's virtue, and a wondrous charm that springs from the artist's state of realization, which is the real spirit of the painting.These qualities can all be used to describe this painting. This is especially true with respect to the pine tree, which was completed with only several simple strokes yet infuses an air of power throughout the entire painting. Moreover, the exquisite and lively little squirrel on the pine trunk was painted using a most wonderful and mysterious technique of the "Fangfa" style of painting. Extraordinary skills were applied to paint it even though its style is plain.

Simplicity, innocent charm, natural appearance, and realness are features of the "Fangfa" style of painting.

This Is How I Determine the Truth (#48)

Artist: H.H. Dorje Chang Buddha III

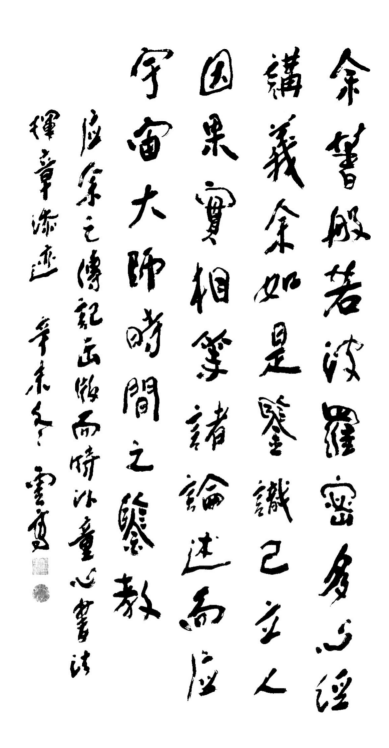

This calligraphic work has its own unique style based on the artist's skills in stone inscriptions. Whether judging from its overall appearance or the manner of brush application, one can see that every stroke contains the prowess of the artist, manifests an amazing appeal, and reflects the holy and pure mind of the artist. This work of calligraphy was Written by H.H. Dorje Chang Buddha III for the publication of His book, *Commentary on the Heart Sutra*. "This Is How I Determine the Truth" and "Know Yourself and Build Your Character" are predictions contained in the book. More than ten years have passed since then. The predictions did become true. This mastery of time in the universe confirmed that Master Wan Ko Yee, as He was known at the time, is actually the highest leader of Buddhism in the world today, H.H. Dorje Chang Buddha III, the author of this calligraphy.

Flying Object in the Night
(#325)

Artist: Yu Hua Shouzhi Wang
Style: Impressionism

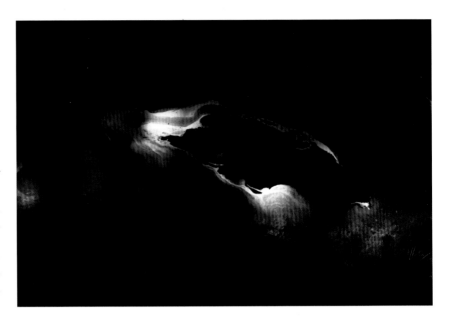

This abstract painting reflects the brightness and vastness of the artist's mind. Against the backdrop of a dark night sky, the charm of the painting's artistic spirit still emerges. The flying object can be thought of as the rhythm of brilliantly leaping ideas. It is neither a flying bird nor a cluster of clouds. Is it the rhythm of the congealing of air? Of course not. Is it the resonation of a shock to the atmosphere? It is not that, either. Is it an alien spaceship? None of these are correct.

In fact, it is a sort of charm – the charm of art and the symbol of the Goddess of Beauty. It originates from the feelings of a vast mind. Executed with extraordinary, seasoned skills, this release of colors can be interpreted in any way. Its artistic value, however, cannot be overlooked. After all, this piece embodies the beauty of art.

Heavenly Treasures in Motion
(#275) (partial picture)

Artist: H.H. Dorje Chang Buddha III
Style: Weiyin

This painting belongs to the "Weiyin" style. The boldly applied colors are bright yet sedate. They convey a strong sense of rhythm and motion, like planets revolving and rotating in the universe. Although the layout is static and unchanging, one is left with the impression that transformations are constantly occurring, producing objects of various forms, such as dragons, phoenixes, water, and fire. The blending of light and darkness creates an interesting scene. Any part of this painting, when enlarged in isolation, is a beautiful work in and of itself.

The style and quality of this painting seem to have originated from a palace of immortals or a heavenly abode. Thus, this painting is titled "Heavenly Treasures in Motion."

Yi Shan Shui Yun Liang Qing Nong (#215)
(One Landscape Charm Presents Two Strong Emotions)

Artist: H.H. Dorje Chang Buddha III
Style: Pomo Weiyun

This is a rare painting that vividly features both splash-ink and splash-color techniques. It belongs to the "Pomo Weiyun" style of painting.

What is meant by "Pomo Weiyun"? It entails bold application of brush and ink, as if the ink is being poured onto the paper. Its appearance is like the traces of a rushing river of thick ink. The natural effect of this technique is beyond description. Within these bold, splashing strokes appear countless minute traces of charm flowing from the watery ink.

This painting portrays a scene of mountains and water as dusk approaches. In it, there is a profound message from a fisherman concerning his enlightenment. The fisherman is telling people: "We should do good deeds, not evil deeds. We should never harm any living being. If you can truly live in such a way, you will enter another world and will realize the truth of neither arising nor ceasing. That would be the most meaningful human existence."

Ni Kan Wo De Jia (See My Home) (#26) (partial picture)

Artist: H.H. Dorje Chang Buddha III
Style: Pomo Xiantiao Xiezhen

Wouldn't you like such a home?

This is a painting in the "Pomo Xiantiao Xiezhen" style. The center brush-tip technique and the side brush-edge technique were both applied in this painting in addition to large-scale freehand brushwork using the splash-ink technique. The mountain scenery was painted with black ink and heavy hues of green. This artwork not only preserves traditional painting skills but also manifests the realistic effect of modern Western oil paintings.

In Chinese paintings, it is very difficult to apply the perspective technique, with its three-dimensional look, to paintings in which the center brush-tip technique is used to express scholarly charm. However, this painting combines four different elements: the three-dimensional perspective technique together with the scattered perspective technique, the splash-ink technique with lines, freehand brushwork, and realism. Attributes from both Chinese and Western paintings form a single stylish charm. The painting is entitled "See My Home." It depicts a pristine rural setting, a land accompanied by mountain, river, sun and moon spirits. One regards a place as home when one has cherished feelings toward the local customs and conditions of that place.

Wan Nian Si (Wan Nian Temple) (#107)

Artist: H.H. Dorje Chang Buddha III
Style: Xiangtong

This painting uses calligraphic techniques to express a natural appeal. The rural ancient temple is depicted with utmost simplicity, as if scribbled by the inexperienced and innocent hand of a child. In reality, however, this work embodies mature artistry. This work belongs to the "Xiantong" style of painting.

Portrait of
a Young Girl (#359)

Artist: Fanny Geefs-Corr
(1807~1883)

A fabulous example of the artist's work, this portrait perfectly illustrates her skills as a painter of portraits and figures. Dating to 1880, Fanny Geefs-Corr has depicted a young girl in the costume of her time holding a bunch of roses. Of particular note is the rather unusual oval format and the presence of a superb original frame.

The artist Fanny Corr was born in Brussels in 1807. As a young girl she studied portrait and figure painting under the guidance of Jean Francois Navez at the Brussels Academy before embarking on a professional career around 1830. Shortly after that she met, and within a couple of years married, the sculptor Guillaume Geefs, and together they established a studio in Brussels. For a while she chose to sign her works 'Fanny Geefs-Corr' but later in life dropped her maiden name from her signature.

She died in Brussels in 1883, but her works are collected by the illustrious Museum of Kortrijk in Belgium and other museums.

Bai Zhang Qun Shan
(Towering Peaks) (#29)

Artist: H.H. Dorje Chang Buddha III

Standing on the golden peak of Mount Emei in 1993, the artist looked down upon all the surrounding peaks. He was free of any attachment or concern. His mind was traveling freely in the universe. That place is truly a blessed land of immortals where people cast off their old self and are reborn. With such a view before him, the artist's mind was not attached to anything. It was in a state of neither coming nor going. After returning home, the artist picked up his brush and casually created this painting. It exemplifies artistic skills born of experience as well as the mindset of an innocent child.

The Turnip Pickers (#343)

Artist: Evariste Carpentier (1845~1922)

Evariste Carpentier was, quite simply, one of the most important Belgian painters of the nineteenth century. His career spanned one of the most exciting periods in the history of European art, and his style changed with the fashions of the time. His early work was much in the traditions of the Salon painters of Germany and France. Paintings from his middle period subtly reflect the influences of Impressionism, and his later pieces clearly illustrate his appreciation for the French 'Plein Air' painters, such as Bastien-Lepage.

Carpentier was born in the small town of Kuurne, Belgium in 1845, and it appears that he showed a precocious talent for the arts. His reputation as one of Belgium's premier painters of rural subjects became well established, and his light-filled images of people at their daily pursuits received enormous critical praise. He joined the art group known as 'XX' (Les Vingt), arguably the most important avant-garde circle of the day, whose purpose was to promote Impressionism and Luminism in Belgium. Evariste Carpentier was, above all, a Luminist whose ability to bathe his paintings in a warm, natural light places him in the forefront of the movement.

His later life was spent in the city of Liege, where he is remembered as the painter who brought Impressionism to that area. In 1897 he became a Professor at the Academy of Liege and from 1902-1919 was its Director. Evariste Carpentier died in Liege in 1922, and his paintings are collected by numerous prominent museums, including the Koninklijk Museum Voor Schone Kunsten, Antwerp, the Musee Royale des Beaux Arts, Brussels and other world class museums.

This highly important example of his work clearly shows the influence of Bastien Lepage. It was painted in Paris, as is evident by the Paris frame maker's label to the reverse, and depicts a family of turnip farmers probably from southern Belgium.

Venus and Putti (#356)

Artist: Daniel Vertangen (1598~1684)

Painting with an exceptional attention to detail, Daniel Vertangen produced some of the finest figure paintings in the Lowlands during the middle of the seventeenth century. His subjects ranged from the mythological to the biblical and from pure portraiture to contemporary landscapes. His figures owe a great deal to the influence of his teacher and mentor, the Utrecht painter Cornelis Van Poelenburgh (1586-1667). As with Van Poelenburgh, his draftsmanship and ability to paint flesh tones are of the highest standards.

Daniel Vertangen was born in the city of The Hague, Holland in 1598. His paintings are highly prized today amongst collectors of Netherlandish paintings of the seventeenth century and are housed in museums throughout the world, including the National Museum of Denmark in Copenhagen and the National Museum of Sweden in Stockholm.

Shu Gen Pen Jing
(Tree Roots Form a Large Bonsai)
(#3)

Artist: H.H. Dorje Chang Buddha III

This painting of plum flowers has the characteristics of nobility, purity, boldness, and vigor. It reveals artistry devoid of the slightest trace of the mundane, manifesting nothing but wondrous appeal. It is free of any rigidity or clumsiness. Such achievement cannot be attained simply by years of diligent work. Rather, it is the crystallization of knowledge and wisdom. This painting has a very special arrangement, and its brush strokes are simple yet skillful. The roots of the plum tree coil around to form what looks like a large bonsai. Embodying both realism and surrealism, this scene conveys a sense of natural loveliness.

After completing this painting, H.H. Dorje Chang Buddha III composed the following poem dedicated to it: "Plum flowers of surpassing loveliness blossom in a pot, though never are they planted. Wave the brush to plant the tree, and the roots of that old tree form their own shallow pot."

Young Girl Seated on
a Marble Bench (#342)

Artist: Pascal de Beucker (1861~1945)

An extremely rare and important example of de Beucker's secular figurative work, this beautifully painted image of a young girl seated on a marble bench dates to 1908, considered his best period. De Beucker is remembered as possibly Belgium's finest painter of still-life subjects at the turn of the twentieth century, and his figure paintings are equally competent.

Pascal de Beucker was born in 1861 in Antwerp, where he studied at the Academy under Farasyn and Lauwers. Upon graduation he commenced exhibiting at a number of Belgium's prominent Salons, winning numerous medals and prizes for his figurative painting. In 1904 he left Belgium for the United States, where he settled in Springfield, Illinois. While in the United States, he became highly sought after for his portraits, which he executed with an attention to detail of the highest quality. In 1910 he returned to Belgium, married and settled in the town of Mortsel and commenced painting the floral compositions for which he is now best known.

Pascal de Beucker continued to paint until his death in 1945. His works have been collected by the Albert van Dyck Museum and other museums. In the year of 2000, a major retrospective of his life and work was held at the Albert van Dyck Museum.

Misty Appeal of a Dilapidated Pond (partial picture)

Artist: H.H. Dorje Chang Buddha III
Style: Thickly Piled Patches of Color

This is a portion of the painting "Misty Appeal of a Dilapidated Pond" created by H.H. Dorje Chang Buddha III. This painting in the Thickly Piled Patches of Color style cohesively combines both impressionism and realism. Our museum possesses only this reproduced portion of the original work. That is why our museum is seeking to purchase from the public original works by H.H. Dorje Chang Buddha III that our museum lacks, such as paintings of water lilies and sunflowers.

Rue de Village (#371)

Artist: Maurice de Vlaminck (1876~1958)

This beautiful example of the work of Maurice de Vlaminck dates from the period of the late 1920's to the early 1930's. Maurice Vlaminck is one of the principal figures in the Fauve movement, a group of modern artists who from 1904 to 1908 were united in their use of intense color. Along with artists such as André Derain and Henri Matisse, Maurice Vlaminck shifted the style of Post-Impressionism into the wildly colorful art of Fauvism.

The sight of Vincent van Gogh's paintings stimulated Vlaminck to begin to paint as a Fauve. His exuberant paint application and vibrant use of color displayed the influence of Vincent van Gogh. In Maurice de Vlaminck's landscape paintings he ignored the details, with the landscape becoming a mere excuse to express mood through violent color and brushwork. Maurice de Vlaminck is best known today for his Fauvism period, a span that lasted about seven years. After a long and illustrious career, Maurice de Vlaminck died in the town of Rueil-La-Gadeliere on October 11th 1958.

Works of Maurice Vlaminck are collected by renowned museums throughout the world, including the Musée d'Orsay in Paris, the Metropolitan Museum of Art in New York, and museums in major cities worldwide.

Jade Panel Painted in Oil Colors - Lake Tai Jade (#312)

Artist: H.H. Dorje Chang Buddha III
Style: Chaoshi

"The heavens shook and beautiful jade descended from high in the clouds. This eye-intoxicating jade in the pattern of a fish belly lay in a dragon's pond. Its charm is like a melody from the cloud palace. The most beautiful flowers throughout the ages pale in comparison."

This jade from the celestial world seems to have descended directly from the high clouds as heaven and earth shook. It seems as if this beautiful, mesmerizing jade from Lake Tai with a charming fish-belly pattern once lay at the bottom of a dragon's pond. With its harmonious mixture of lightness and opaqueness, it is like a wonderful melody bestowed upon the human world from a treasure palace high in the clouds. It displays a tone of utmost attractiveness. From the time Lake Tai Jade appeared in this world, the patterns, lines, and spots on all other beautiful stones suddenly lost their glamour, just as a flower of utmost beauty loses it glamour. However, this stirring yet comforting Lake Tai Jade of unsurpassed beauty and charming colors is not a creation of nature. Rather, it originated from brushwork in the "Chaoshi" style.

Jade Panel Painted in Oil Colors - Coral-Red Jade (#310)

Artist: H.H. Dorje Chang Buddha III
Style: Chaoshi

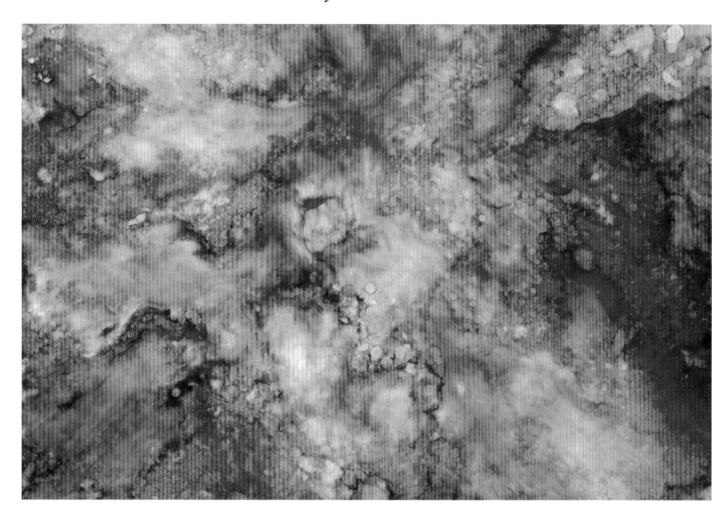

"A folk song handed down says that of all jade, the coral-red type is the rarest in the world." This is referring to coral-red jade, a rare treasure in this world indeed. Throughout the vast expanse of history, the existence of coral-red jade has been passed down by word of mouth. Coral-red jade thus became like an ancient, beautiful legend only known in people's memories but almost never seen in the world.

Now, thanks to the painting and sculpting skills of H.H. Dorje Chang Buddha III, people of the world are finally able to see the true appearance of coral-red jade. It looks like coral flowers under the sea but also has the loveliness of a pinkish jade. People say that Indian red is classy, beautiful, and elegant. However, Indian red is truly unworthy even to accompany coral-red jade. The beauty of any building material or building stones used in this world can in no way compare with the beauty of coral-red jade. If a panel of coral-red jade is laid in the center of a living room or lounge, then it truly would be as the ancients described: "The myriad delicately sculpted flowers of exceptional beauty are all ashamed once the resplendent appearance of coral-red jade is present."

From where does this splendid color that brings people happiness come? Of course, it was painted using techniques of the "Chaoshi" style created by H.H. Dorje Chang Buddha III. A poem composed by H.H. Dorje Chang Buddha III reads, "Looking over this stone on the ground, underlying its colors is maha (greatness)." Those with understanding know that all of these hues contain a maha realm, a realm of greatness. The word "maha" or "greatness" here gives people much food for thought!

Jade Panel Painted in Oil Colors - Sea-Reef Jade (#313)

Artist: H.H. Dorje Chang Buddha III
Style: Chaoshi

Where in this human world can such an extraordinary, unique, wondrous, and beautiful stone be found? It presumably is a reef rock composed of brownish sand that came from the depths of the sea. It has holes that seem to be from water erosion and appears to have partially vaporized due to temperature changes. The undulating ridges on its surface seem to be traces of contact with huge waves. It looks like a reef at a first glance, yet it has an obvious watery tone. It is extraordinary, magical, and extremely beautiful. Looking more closely with a concentrated mind, you will see layer upon layer at different depths and endless alternations of emptiness and substance. The pattern is elegant, manifesting thousands of variations that presumably could only be created from weather erosion and geological processes. A boundless world is indeed revealed in this one piece!

Such jade is actually a treasure that exists only in the Dragon King's palace and can never be found in the human world. Its recreation in this world can only be accomplished through the painting wonders of H.H. Dorje Chang Buddha III, whose poem in honor of this jade translates as, "Reef jade is rare even in the depths of the sea. How difficult it is to find no matter how deep you go. Mountain-high waves impacted this magical stone. Smiling, broad-minded, I reveal the essence of painting." Without abundant talent, who could compose such elegant poetry, not to mention create the "Chaoshi" style of painting?

Jade Panel Painted in Oil Colors - Lotus Pattern Jade (#309)

Artist: H.H. Dorje Chang Buddha III
Style: Chaoshi

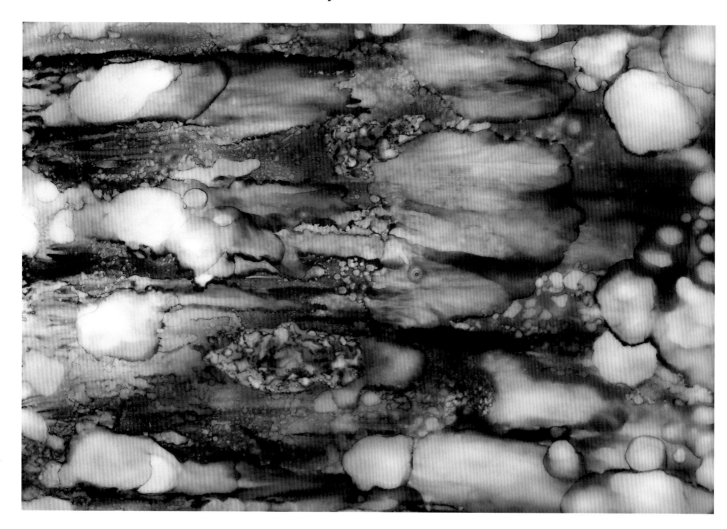

"Speaking of the most famous marble, it would be marble with the patterns of duckweed and seeds inside lotus pods. Such marble cannot be unearthed in mountains or valleys. Its superb exquisiteness can only be produced through ink." This poem composed by H.H. Dorje Chang Buddha III refers to a marble-like jade called "Lotus Pattern Jade."

What is the most famous and precious type of marble? That would of course be marble "with the patterns of duckweed and seeds inside lotus pods." The patterns on the surface of such gemstones may resemble those of duckweed floating near lotus flowers. Such patterns may also have the air of lotus pod seeds that fuzzily float up and down, which patterns are most rare. Marble with these patterns can be regarded as gemstones of which even those in heaven would be proud. However, you will not find such treasures even if you traverse the entire earth with all of its mountains, waters, land, and continents. That is why the poem states, "Such marble cannot be unearthed in mountains or valleys. Its superb exquisiteness can only be produced through ink." Only through the brushwork of H.H. Dorje Chang Buddha III and His application of the "Chaoshi" technique can such a uniquely exquisite Lotus Pattern Jade be created for all to see.

Painting Tiles (#314)

Artist: H.H. Dorje Chang Buddha III   Style: Chaoshi

When you see these four tiles with gemstone patterns, it seems there is nothing more to say other than they give you a feeling of beauty and naturalness. However, as soon as you realize they are actually four paintings, you will marvel at them in a state of perplexity. All of them are indeed paintings in patterns of jade. They are representative of works that belong to the "Chaoshi" style of painting. Starting clockwise from the top left, they are Dragon-Scale Jade, Autumn Aqueous, Fortune Vase Jade, and Yellow Loveliness Jade. Their patterns, watery tone, luster, and moist appearance are completely the same as those of natural jade objects. Such accomplishment clearly shows the calligraphic and painting mastery of H.H. Dorje Chang Buddha III in the style of "Chaoshi."

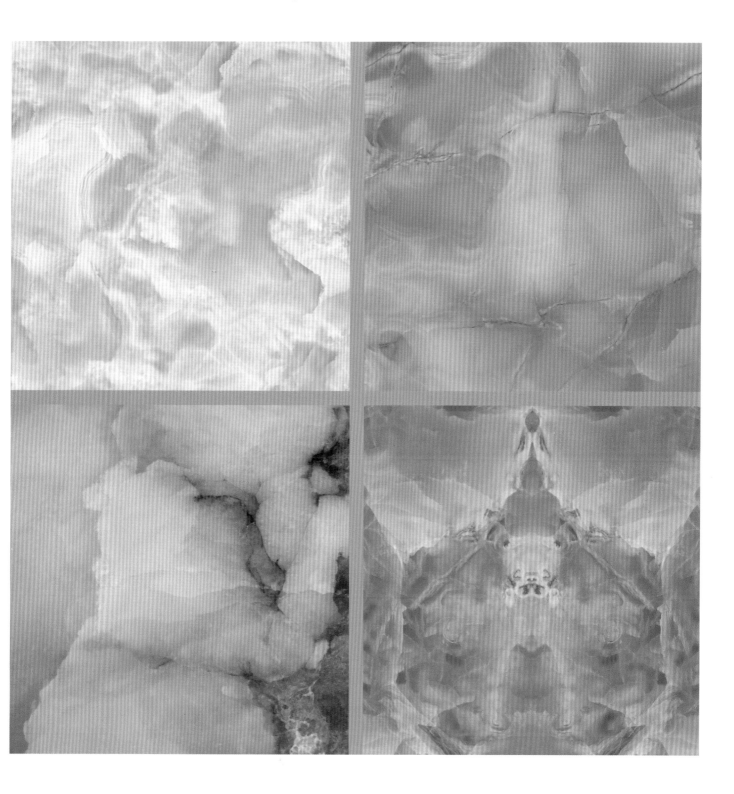

Reishi Mushroom Art Frame (#317)

Artist: H.H. Dorje Chang Buddha III

This faux reishi mushroom art frame was sculpted and painted with oil colors by H.H. Dorje Chang Buddha III. It captures the form and texture of reishi mushrooms (Ganoderma lucidum) and has the gracefulness of an aged cultural relic. This art frame embodies artistry that is quite fascinating.

Sheep-Tallow Jade Art Frame (#287)

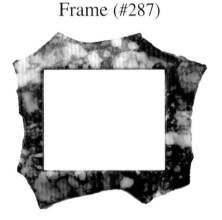

Artist: H.H. Dorje Chang Buddha III

This is a faux sheep-tallow jade art frame sculpted and painted by H.H. Dorje Chang Buddha III. It has the pattern, color, watery tone, and texture of real jade.

White Jade Gingko-Root Art Frame (#320)

Artist: H.H. Dorje Chang Buddha III

This is a faux white jade ginkgo-root art frame sculpted and painted by H.H. Dorje Chang Buddha III. In addition to having the pattern, color, and texture of natural ginkgo tree roots, it also has the watery tone of real white jade.

Natural Tree-Root Art Frame (#321)

Artist: H.H. Dorje Chang Buddha III

This is a faux natural tree-root art frame sculpted and painted by H.H. Dorje Chang Buddha III. It has the pattern, color, and texture of real tree roots.

Root-Artistry Art Frame (#324)

Artist: H.H. Dorje Chang Buddha III

This is a faux root-artistry art frame sculpted and painted by H.H. Dorje Chang Buddha III. It has the pattern, color, and texture of natural tree roots.

Emerald-Jade Art Frame (#285)

Artist: H.H. Dorje Chang Buddha III

This is a faux emerald-jade art frame sculpted and painted by H.H. Dorje Chang Buddha III. It has the pattern, color, watery tone, and texture of real jade.

Pendant Stone Art Frame (#327)

Artist: H.H. Dorje Chang Buddha III

Sculpted and painted by H.H. Dorje Chang Buddha III, this art frame depicts the look of gray-black white-spotted granite. It expresses the open, rugged feelings of ethnic cultures as well as a simple, unadorned country air.

Eight Auspicious Symbols Art Frame (#328)

Artist: H.H. Dorje Chang Buddha III

This art frame was sculpted and painted by H.H. Dorje Chang Buddha III. Seven gemstones combine with one foundation stone to form the eight auspicious symbols. Accompanied by rough cords and wooden rods, this frame is expressive of the simple culture of native peoples. A regal aura blends with a rustic flavor, rendering the frame at once pristine and grand. The innovative concept of the piece enables it to exude a subtle elegance.

Art Frame of Withered Vines on an Intoxicating Stone (#306)

Artist: H.H. Dorje Chang Buddha III

From ancient times to the present, the art of making frames has existed in the East, the West, regions of different nationalities, among the general population and within imperial palaces. Each of these types of artistic frames has its own features and advantages. However, only Yun frames can truly be called painting frames that embody consummate artistry. Among Yun frames, "Withered Vines on an Intoxicating Stone" is the acme of painting-frame artistry. It is said that a painting is easy to acquire, but a Yun frame is so difficult to obtain. Naturally, Yun frames have become peerless treasures. Usually, the frame sets off the painting. However, with the frame "Withered Vines on an Intoxicating Stone," the situation is totally opposite—the painting sets off the frame. Simply put, the worth and prestige of any painting mounted to this frame will increase tremendously.

This art frame has an air of simple elegance, purity, and understated charm. It naturally captures the spirit and form of real withered vines. Both faux withered vines and faux ancient jade are first sculpted using Yun Sculpture techniques and then painted in oils. Withered vines sculpted by H.H. Dorje Chang Buddha III are of the highest artistic quality and possess the following four special characteristics for the viewer's appreciation: (1) Their appeal is aptly described by four words: old, withered, dry, and beautiful. (2) Their style embodies four attributes: scholarliness, absence of mediocrity, high elegance, and a comforting air. (3) Their form and design present four properties: coiling in a natural way, totally genuine appearance, weathered over time, and intertwining. (4) Their texture has four unique features: the texture of having withered in different time periods; the texture of real vines with tiny pores; the lines and wrinkles follow the natural course of the vines; and the colors and appearances are just like those of real ancient vines.

Among these characteristics, the four unique features of texture are most important for determining whether a work of art is a genuine, top-grade sculpture of withered vines. These four unique features are the most important criteria by which to judge whether a work of faux withered vines was hand-sculpted by H.H. Dorje Chang Buddha III. The first of these four unique features is that the vines have the texture of having withered in different time periods. Since real intertwined withered vines come into being and grow in different time periods, they dry, age, and shrivel to different degrees. Their colors also vary. Thus, faux vines must give the impression of being historical relics of different time periods.

The second of these four unique features is that the vines have the texture of real vines with tiny pores. That is, the texture of the faux vines, including the stems and skin, will look exactly like those of real vines. Even under the scrutiny of a magnifying glass, wonderful subtleties of the faux vines will be revealed. Not only must the texture of the faux vines be no different from that of real vines, the faux vines must also be much more beautiful than real vines.

The third of these four unique features is that the lines and wrinkles follow the natural course of the vines. The texture of faux vines will be the same as that of ancient vines which show aged wrinkles formed over a vast expanse of time. The lines on the faux vines will match the vine on which they appear. As the vines change directions, these lines will follow the twists and turns. They must look natural and no different from real lines on ancient vines.

The fourth of these four unique features is that the colors and appearance are just like those of real ancient vines. The colors of the sculpted vines will have an ancient charm. Such vines will appear old, parched, and shriveled, but in a fascinating and attractive way. They will not show any trace of having been sculpted by man. They will be devoid of all of the freshness and brightness of living vines, appearing as relics that are at least a thousand years old.

Only those art frames that possess all of the above-described distinguishing characteristics can be called authentic, peerless art frames of faux withered vines hand-sculpted by H.H. Dorje Chang Buddha III.

Mysterious Mist Inside a Stone (#316)

Artist: H.H. Dorje Chang Buddha III

Yun Sculpture

The external appearance of this stone is too beautiful to be absorbed all at once. It looks like a rough unearthed stone that contains jade. It is therefore no ordinary stone. Inside of it is a world filled with mystery! It belongs to the "Yun Sculpture" form of art, a unique form of sculpture created by H.H. Dorje Chang Buddha III. His Holiness the Buddha is the sole founder of this mysterious form of carving. In creating this wondrous art form, He has opened up an entirely new epoch in the history of art in this world.

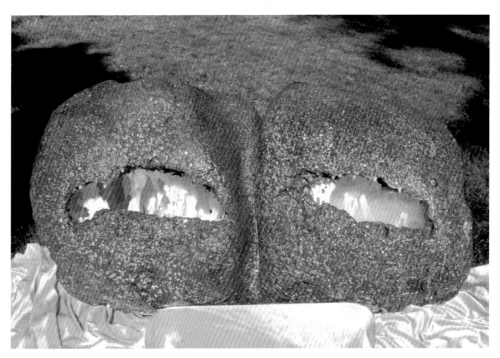

In the history of human art, artists have displayed to the world art they created that reflected their particular artistic strengths. They thereby added to people's aesthetic enjoyment and enriched civilization. However, after evaluation, art experts have unanimously agreed that Yun Sculpture created by H.H. Dorje Chang Buddha III is the most marvelous and astonishing form of art in the history of human civilization. Such sculptures appear even more natural than the superlative craftsmanship of nature itself. Moreover, it is the first type of art in this world that is impossible to duplicate. The worth of this precious faux boulder is truly astounding. A certain organization offered to buy it for US$70,000,000; however, H.H. Dorje Chang Buddha III politely refused the offer.

Let us look at this mysterious oval stone. From its external appearance, one can see that "Mysterious Mist Inside a Stone" is an ordinary greenish rock that is a few feet long. However, the inside of it is a totally different world. Its interior contains layer upon layer of what appears to be peaks and hills, forming a beautiful crisscrossing network. Its scenes seem to change endlessly, giving it a profoundly mystical quality. It contains multiple layers, and its mysterious structure has caused those who view it to be lost in astonishment. In some parts of the stone's interior, there is mist as exquisite as chiffon, while in other parts the mist is so thick it covers whatever is behind it. In the latter case, a lamplight that penetrates mist must be shone into the stone to view the background scenes. One can see mist circling upward. This carving even surpasses the work of nature itself.

In this world, the goal of artists is to create natural-looking works of art. However, the carvings of H.H. Dorje Chang Buddha III excel nature. Natural limestone caves, stones, and mountain ranges cannot compare with the sculptures of H.H. Dorje Chang Buddha III. Moreover, sculptors throughout history have been able to produce material forms or images through sculpting. However, no one has been able to produce through sculpting something as insubstantial and formless as fog or mist. Nonetheless, there are sculptures of H.H. Dorje Chang Buddha III that combine both material form and mist.

That is why when experts evaluate such works of art they sincerely praise them as that which could not possibly come from this earthly realm. They say that only something from another world could be so marvelous and unbelievable. They conclude that the sculptures of H.H. Dorje Chang Buddha III are the only true masterpieces of art in the world today that surpass even nature itself!

As the poem that H.H. Dorje Chang Buddha III composed for "Mysterious Mist Inside a Stone" says, "White jade-like gauze hangs inside a stone. Unmatched sculpting produces emotion amid the mist. Without words, a rare melody plays inside the cave. Such heavenly scenery is difficult to duplicate."

Forever Brilliant (#22) (partial picture)

Artist: H.H. Dorje Chang Buddha III

Yun Sculpture

This Yun Sculpture art is called "Forever Brilliant." This unmatched form of art was created for the first time in this human world by H.H. Dorje Chang Buddha III. In so doing, H.H. Dorje Chang Buddha III pioneered for the first time in human history a form of art whose works cannot be duplicated by any person or through any scientific method. Such unprecedented art is truly mysterious. Yun Sculpture art is inexhaustibly beautiful and extremely mystical. These works of art are like treasures from heaven. An astronomical telescope once captured a portion of the planet Mars, which appeared like Yun Sculpture art in both structure and color. However, that portion of Mars was not as elegant and natural-looking as Yun Sculpture art. That is why such art is called treasures from heaven.

The basic materials of Yun sculptures are stone, wood, acrylic, and oil colors. The sculptures are made by combining the two techniques of carving and hand-molding. The final step in the process is applying a variety of oil colors, such as red, orange, yellow, green, and blue, into one integral whole. This form of art integrates the two aspects of sculpting and painting. Such beautiful, precious art is unique in the entire world. As experts have stated, since the appearance of Yun Sculpture art, "all of the world's most gorgeous jewels and jade have been outshone and pale in comparison, just like the stars that surround a bright moon." The beauty of Yun sculptures is truly riveting.

At a special Yun Sculpture exhibition held by the United States Congress, visitors praised the exhibits with words such as, "These are gifts that God gave to mankind!" All we can do is use the following several words to express the profound significance of this precious art that seems to have come from heaven: unique, alive, extraordinary, beautiful, elegant, charming, wondrous, and magical.

Ancient Withered Vines Become a Fossil Fortress (#283)

Artist: H.H. Dorje Chang Buddha III

Yun Sculpture

H.H. Dorje Chang Buddha III created this work through sculpting followed by oil painting. The techniques used to make it are those used to make Yun sculptures. The main theme of this sculpture is ancient vines that have fossilized through the ages. Superior skills are revealed from the winding of the vines and the carving inside the hollow interior of the stone. This artwork not only has the charming look of a natural stone, it also has an elegance born of artistic design. All artwork by H.H. Dorje Chang Buddha III comes from the same source. Each is an original creation unprecedented in history.

Holy Purity (#315) (partial picture)

Artist: H.H. Dorje Chang Buddha III

Yun Sculpture

"Holy Purity" is one of the works in the category of Yun Sculpture, a precious form of art of unsurpassed beauty created by H.H. Dorje Chang Buddha III. Yun sculptures are works of art that cannot be duplicated by any person or any scientific technology, which is unprecedented in human history. With the advent of Yun Sculpture, non-replicable artwork has finally appeared in this world. Yun sculptures exhibit graceful variations at multiple levels. Their beauty is both astonishing and spellbinding. The two skills of sculpting and painting are embodied in each one of them. The structures of Yun sculptures are both exquisitely fine and complicated, with unanticipated variations. To say that Yun sculptures are the most wonderful works of art is simply insufficient.

Take, for example, this sculpture called "Holy Purity." Its color is soft and lustrous, like thin white silk. It looks as pure and noble as jade or ice, has an elegant hanging style, and is completely free of any flaw. This artwork that is pleasing to the eye and comforting to the mind fully deserves that name it was given, for it indeed possesses the qualities of holiness, purity, elegance, refinement, and white splendor.

At an exhibition held at the United States Capitol, visitors praised the Yun Sculpture exhibits with words such as, "These are gifts that God gave to mankind!" A sense of moistness appears from the white, the only color used to create it.

Like a jade lock or a small bell, this sculpture seems to hold emotions within it. Beauty of this type is so difficult to achieve in the human world. This is the only supra-mundane, holy, pure, artwork in the entire world that is as white as icy jade, as wondrous as heavenly sounds, and as beautiful as a celestial valley.

Universe in Motion
(#282)

Artist: H.H. Dorje Chang
Buddha III
Style: Chaoshi

Yun Sculpture

The natural stone-pattern effect of "Universe in Motion" was achieved by painting it only after it was fully sculpted. The painting technique belongs to the "Chaoshi" style. The arrangement and shape of this Yun sculpture are quite marvelous. The lines are so simple, distinctive, and flowing. Each angle you view it from will give you a considerably different impression. There is a type of inner-force that spirals from top to bottom and from left to right. This dynamic force of nature seems to enable us to see the center of the universe. This is the melody of life. That is why another name for this artwork is "Melody." What do we want to say here after all? Actually, only one word—art.

119

(#302)

Parched Ancient Coral (#302)

Artist: Yu Hua Shouzhi Wang

"Parched Ancient Coral" was hand-sculpted and painted in oil colors by Professor Yu Hua Shouzhi Wang. Its shape and colors are even more genuine-looking and beautiful than those of real coral from the bottom of the sea or parched islands. When touching this sculpture, it obviously feels like coral that has been eroded through immersion in water. One cannot help but marvel that Yu Hua Shouzhi Wang has recreated through her brushwork coral with the texture of having been soaked and eroded for millions of years. Such coral is difficult to find even at the bottom of the sea. Its appeal is even further enhanced with the matching hand-sculpted vase called "Lucui Qilang (Emerald Green Fine Jade)." This entire hand-sculpted and hand-painted faux coral has an air of elegance and refinement, surpassing the beauty of natural coral. With unparalleled works of art such as this, it is no wonder the artistic accomplishments of Yu Hua Shouzhi Wang were recognized as "treasures of the world." (Please see the United States Congressional Record for details.)

Sheep Tallow Dew (#303)

Artist: Yu Hua Shouzhi Wang

Pink, moist-looking, and with understated luster, this faux coral seems as sleek as sheep tallow jade. It conveys a sense of morning dew that is deeply moving. Its wonder, colors, lustrous beauty, overall quality, and artistic flair unite to form a precious sculpture captivating in both spirit and appearance. People call it "Sheep Tallow Dew." Combined with a hand-sculpted, delightful, elegant matching vase of milky white faux jade, it becomes a doubly charming masterpiece.

When a special exhibition of the art of Yu Hua Shouzhi Wang was held at the United States Capitol, it was concluded in the Congressional Record that her wood-based faux coral and cobblestones that she hand-sculpted and painted with oil colors "have become treasures of the world." This fact is undeniable. Her highly elegant and exceedingly beautiful faux corals are truly not to be found anywhere else in the world. Yu Hua Shouzhi Wang is the sole successful creator of sculpted and painted faux coral and faux cobblestones in this world.

Hanging Coral (#307)

Artist: Yu Hua Shouzhi Wang

This attractively hanging coral, which is as white as white jade, is called "Hanging Coral." After it was sculpted from a wood material, it was painted with oil colors and glazed. Most importantly, it conveys a sense of moistness and distinctive texture stemming from its natural-looking shape, hues, and luster. It is sleek yet true to life, as if it were real coral. All who view it will enjoy its purity, elegance, and comforting air. Combined with the matching vase called "Cai Yi Tao," this faux coral appears even more beautiful than its real counterpart in nature and even more attractive and elegant. This sculpture was displayed at a special exhibition of the art of Yu Hua Shouzhi Wang (Dr. Yu Hua Wang) held at the United States Capitol in 2008.

(#307)

(#303)

120

Sea Palace Monarch
(#300)

Artist: Yu Hua Shouzhi Wang

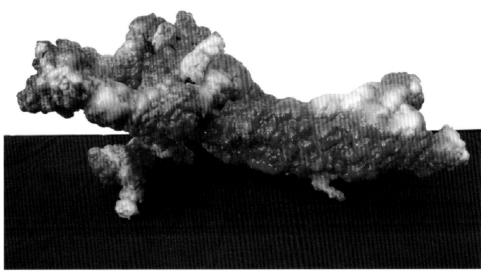

This gigantic coral you now see has been named "Sea Palace Monarch." Presumably, your first feeling was that of surprise. Is it a genuine coral? Does such large coral exist in the world? If it is not a genuine coral, then why do its luster, texture, and appearance look so real and natural? From the bottom of your heart, you would happily accept it as genuine coral because it is truly so beautiful, so aesthetically pleasing. How beautiful your living room would be if it contained this sculpture! Nonetheless, reason and knowledge tell you that this world could not possibly have genuine coral so huge and so gorgeous. Indeed, even if you searched every corner of every coral reef in the oceans of the earth, you would still not find coral of such beauty and size. Its name, "Sea Palace Monarch," means that it is the sovereign of the seas since it is the largest treasure in all the oceans. However, such colossal and splendid coral cannot be found in real oceans because it simply does not exist in this world.

It was created by Dr. Yu Hua Shouzhi Wang using wood that she hand-sculpted and painted in oil colors. The objects that she paints are completely genuine looking. In particular, the texture, watery tone, colors, and charm of her faux coral sculptures look entirely real. Actually, such sculptures are even more beautiful than real coral.

Mouse-Fur-Pattern Coral, Green Coral, Yellow Coral (#301)

Artist: Yu Hua Shouzhi Wang

Each of these three faux coral sculptures has its own distinct allure and shades of color. The aged appearance of the mouse-fur-pattern faux coral gives it the particularly strong charm of an ancient fossil from the deep sea. However, the green faux coral, which seems permeable to light, looks as if it was taken from the waters near Malaysia and Indonesia. It was painted in vivid water colors and conveys sublime elegance. Its delightful spring green expresses purity and freshness. The yellow faux coral resembling fine jade reveals an inner warmth that would certainly be enjoyable to the touch. Each of these three works is an embodiment of talent in sculpting and painting.

  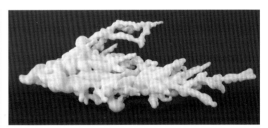

SIXTEEN STYLES OF PAINTING AND PURCHASE OF PAINTINGS

After viewing the exhibits on display at the International Art Museum of America, many people mention that paintings created by H.H. Dorje Chang Buddha III, which are among those exhibits, are divided into fifteen different styles of painting. They want to have a more detailed understanding of those fifteen styles of painting. Therefore, we provide below a brief introduction to those different styles.

The achievements of H.H. Dorje Chang Buddha III are myriad. Let us put aside for now twenty-nine of the thirty large categories of achievements contained in the book *H.H. Dorje Chang Buddha III*. With respect to only one of those thirty large categories—painting achievements—H.H. Dorje Chang Buddha III has founded sixteen different styles of painting. This is in addition to being able to paint paintings of all other currently existing schools, such as the realist, abstractionist, and impressionist schools. The sixteen distinctive styles of painting that H.H. Dorje Chang Buddha III has independently created are as follows: 1. The "Chaoshi" style; 2. The "Chouxiang Yunwei" style; 3. The "Wenfeng" style; 4. The "Fangfa" style; 5. The "Menglong" style; 6. The "Xiangtong" style 7. The "Fanjuan" style; 8. The "Pomo Xiantiao Xiezhen" style; 9. The "Weiyin" style; 10. The "Fanpu" style; 11. The "Miaoxie" style; 12. The "Pomo Weiyun" style; 13. The "Kuangxi" style; 14. The "Yousi" style; 15. The "Banqi" style; and 16. The "Thickly Piled Patches of Color" style.

H.H. Dorje Chang Buddha III has an extremely serious attitude toward the art of calligraphy and painting. Although He has painted more than10,000 paintings, He has nonetheless burned up almost all of them. As long as H.H. Dorje Chang Buddha III is dissatisfied with a painting He painted, He will surely burn it up. There have been numerous occasions when He openly burned up His paintings, including those that were already nicely mounted. Such is the unusual conduct of one with a sense of responsibility toward art. It has been determined through investigation that there are now only 197 authentic paintings by H.H. Dorje Chang Buddha III that exist in the world.

Nevertheless, the International Art Museum of America is also unsurpassed in the entire world in the variety and number of authentic paintings by H.H. Dorje Chang Buddha III that it has collected and displayed. However, at the present time (June of 2011), our museum still has not collected paintings of the sixteenth style of painting called "Thickly Piled Patches of Color." Our museum is also somewhat deficient in a small portion of the other fifteen styles of painting. Additionally, as the inherently highest leader of Buddhism in the history of Buddhism, H.H. Dorje Chang Buddha III is busy benefiting living beings and performing Buddhist matters, and thus has no time to paint. Furthermore, H.H. Dorje Chang Buddha III has clearly refused to ever accept a request from the International Art Museum of America to purchase from Him any of His works of art.

Therefore, our museum has decided to purchase paintings by H.H. Dorje Chang Buddha III from art collectors in society. However, as the value of paintings by H.H. Dorje Chang Buddha III has risen, numerous counterfeit paintings have appeared in society. Many of these counterfeit paintings are stamped with seals that H.H. Dorje Chang Buddha III previously used. Such seals were stolen from H.H. Dorje Chang Buddha III in 2001. Consequently, it is difficult to differentiate counterfeit paintings from authentic paintings. That is why the International Art Museum of America has established strict inspection procedures for its purchase of any painting by H.H. Dorje Chang Buddha III.

Our museum will purchase any authentic painting by H.H. Dorje Chang Buddha III that is stamped with His three-dimensional fingerprint seal (either on the front or back of the painting) and is a type of painting our museum is deficient in or does not have. The purchase price for such a painting will be US$300,000 to US$900,000 per square foot, depending on the level or grade of the painting. Our museum will purchase any oil painting by H.H. Dorje Chang Buddha III that belongs to the "Thickly Piled Patches of Color" style of painting that He founded. Whether such a painting is one of scenery or one of flowers and plants, its purchase price will be US$1,000,000 per square foot. However, if it is a sunflower or water lily painting in the "Thickly Piled Patches of Color" style, as long as it is proven to be an authentic painting signed by H.H. Dorje Chang Buddha III, whether or not it has a fingerprint seal, its purchase price will be more than US$1,000,000 per square foot.

Those willing to sell any such paintings that they themselves have collected should first mail to the International Art Museum of America a photograph of the painting. The three-dimensional fingerprint seal on the painting should be enlarged to at least two square inches. After an initial evaluation of the photograph is made, notice will be given to examine the painting itself. In that examination, no evaluation or recommendation from an artist whose works are exhibited at the International Art Museum of America will be accepted. Only experts hired by the museum will examine and determine the authenticity and price of all such paintings.

The following is a brief introduction to the sixteen styles of painting created by H.H. Dorje Chang Buddha III:

1. **The "Chaoshi" style**
   Such paintings are even more lifelike, appealing, detailed, and beautiful than the actual subjects they portray.

2. **The "Chouxiang Yunwei" style**
   The true appearance of the subject portrayed is changed in these captivating ink-wash paintings, resulting in an unconventional image that both looks like yet does not look like the actual subject.

3. **The "Wenfeng" style**
   Brushwork skills suggestive of scholarliness and poetic charm embody these paintings.

4. **The "Fangfa" style**
   This delightful painting style is lively yet natural, producing a dynamic and fascinating effect from scattered ink.

5. **The "Menglong" style**
   Realism and non-realism are combined to capture the image of the subject portrayed, resulting in a seeming likeness but actual non-likeness of the subject. Brush strokes and color application produce a strong fanciful look to these paintings, a lovely, hazy look in which the real and the surreal mingle.

6. **The "Xiangtong" style**
   There is a rustic and childlike charm to these paintings. With the mindset of an innocent child, the artist casually wields his brush without being led by pre-conceived notions, applying a seasoned adeptness that conveys an impression of simplicity and purity.

7. **The "Fanjuan" style**
   Numerous strokes of the brush reveal an air of scholarliness. Although a myriad of brush strokes are applied, there is no sense of disorder; rather, artistic talent based on profound and extensive knowledge is expressed.

8. **The "Pomo Xiantiao Xiezhen" style**
   The splash-ink technique is merged with the center brush-tip technique to create realistic paintings of landscapes.

9. **The "Weiyin" style**
   These impressionist paintings have reached such a high level that if any small portion of the full painting were isolated, it would be an exquisite impressionist painting in and of itself. These paintings express a dreamy, illusory state, and any small part of them can be enlarged to form its own beautiful, aesthetically enjoyable painting.

10. **The "Fanpu" style**
    These paintings express the artistic conception of returning to original purity and simplicity. With unfettered hand and mind, the artist applies his most mature skills free of the slightest attachment and with minimal, natural strokes of the brush.

11. **The "Miaoxie" style**
    Subtle, fine brushwork and freehand brushwork blend into one. White lines are formed through the delicate, refined, marvelous application of ink rather than through the use of white paint. The artist produces the effect of a realistic painting with meticulous attention to detail even though He applies the freehand style.

12. **The "Pomo Weiyun" style**
    Although bold and vigorous hues of watery ink are used, a rich charm is evinced that is both subtle and wonderful.

13. **The "Kuangxi" style**
    Such paintings fuse rough and precise artistry. The roughest, most rigid, most vigorous brush strokes of the large-scale freehand style are masterfully combined with the fine, delicate brush strokes of the realistic style, resulting in elegance amid roughness.

14. **The "Yousi" style**
    Mostly applied in figure painting, this technique uses gossamer-like fine lines to form the contours of the subject.

15. **The "Banqi" style**
    Such paintings appear to be in the style of those imprinted from engraved plates, but they also manifest the flair of the brush. Deep within them is an inexhaustibly enchanting quality that is both natural and lively. They are ink-wash paintings, not paintings imprinted from engraved plates.

16. **The "Thickly Piled Patches of Color" style**
    Thickly applied oil colors are piled up, giving the painting a three-dimensional look with elegant, vigorous charm. The overall effect is produced through rough brushwork and a sense of surrealism.

有關十六個畫派及收購徵集作品

很多人在美國國際藝術館看到了陳列的展品，提到其中有第三世多杰羌佛創作的作品分爲十五個畫派，他們想更多地了解具體的十五個畫派，爲此在這裏特作一簡單介紹。第三世多杰羌佛創造的成就是非常之多的，我們撇開列在《多杰羌佛第三世》書中的三十個大類成就中的二十九類不説，只就三十大類之一繪畫的成就，即有十六個畫派，除了能畫具象、抽象、印象等派之外，自己創造了十六個不同的畫派，分別名爲：1.超實派；2.抽象韻味派；3.文風派；4.放發派；5.朦朧派；6.鄉童派；7.繁卷派；8.潑墨線條寫真派；9.微印派；10.返璞派；11.妙寫派；12.潑墨微韻派；13.獷細派；14.游絲派；15.版氣派；16.厚堆色塊派。

第三世多杰羌佛對書畫藝術的態度是極其認真嚴肅的，他畫過上萬張畫，但基本上都把它們用火燒掉了，只要是第三世多杰羌佛認爲不滿意的作品，必然火燒，曾經有很多次公開燒畫，包括精裝裱好了的也一火燒之，這是對藝術負責的奇特舉動。目前考證，流傳在世界上的真跡繪畫只有一百九十七張，儘管如此，本館收藏陳列展出的第三世多杰羌佛的真跡繪畫在全世界也是最完整和最多的。但是，第十六個"厚堆色塊派"目前（2011年6月）爲止，還沒有收藏到一幅作品，其它派風格也有少部分的作品欠缺。加之第三世多杰羌佛是世界佛教史以來固有的最高佛教領袖，爲利衆生，法務繁忙，沒有時間繪畫，並且第三世多杰羌佛已明確永久拒絕美國國際藝術館向他購買作品的要求，因此我館現決定向社會收藏家們徵購。但是，由于隨着第三世多杰羌佛的書畫價格的升高，社會上出現了很多仿冒品，這些仿冒品有很多蓋的是第三世多杰羌佛以前用的圖章，而這些圖章早在2001年就被他人竊取，因此造成真假難分，所以，美國國際藝術館對收購的第三世多杰羌佛的畫作，有嚴謹的審查程序。凡屬於第三世多杰羌佛繪畫真跡、蓋有立體指紋印（在書畫的畫面或背面）者、爲本館所缺空之作品，本館將根據作品的級別，以每一平方英尺30萬至90萬美金收購。凡屬於第三世多杰羌佛創始的"厚堆色塊派"油畫作品，無論是風景或者花卉，以每平方英尺100萬美金收購。如果畫的是向日葵或睡蓮，只要證明是真跡且題了款的，並不一定需要蓋有指紋印，則以每平方英尺100萬美金以上商談收購。有願意將自己收藏作品貢獻者，請先寄畫的照片，並將立體指紋印放大到2平方英寸，在初核後再予通知鑑定原作，對收購作品的審核，不接受任何在美國國際藝術館陳列有展品的藝術家的鑑定和推薦，一律由美國國際藝術館請專家審核、裁定並作估價。

下面即是第三世多杰羌佛創始的十六個畫派的簡略說明。

1. 超實派－－比真實境的更真、更情調，質感更強、更細微、更美。

2. 抽象韻味派－－把真實形象變態，以水墨氣韻得到脫俗的是與不是之象。

3. 文風派－－帶文人書卷氣，具有文人書香詩情卷氣的筆上書寫畫功夫。

4. 放發派－－放發神韻天成，墨氣活而自然，生發出動態的放發墨韻效果享受。

5. 朦朧派－－即是以虛實幻化筆意取物造型，得其似是而非，在筆觸和色韻上產生強烈的虛無縹緲筆意、虛實不定的朦朧狀的筆情墨趣。

6. 鄉童派－－具鄉土童心味，用樸實純凈的老辣功夫，以孩童心境隨意無牽而落筆。

7. 繁卷派－－以繁多的筆觸展顯書卷氣效果，其萬千繁筆而不亂，出顯學識淵博的才華。

8. 潑墨線條寫真派－－用潑墨結合中鋒線條書寫技法爲一體，畫出真山真水真貌。

9. 微印派－－爲印象派風格，同時達到大幅畫中任取其中一小部分也是精緻的印象畫，表現精神夢幻中的感覺意境，每一小塊局部放大都是一幅美麗的享受。

10. 返璞派－－即是返璞歸真之意境，以最成熟的功夫放手解心，毫不着意，寥寥信手，自然隨筆。

11. 妙寫派－－是微妙工筆相融寫意爲一體，用微細而脫俗奇妙的黑墨變白線筆觸，而不是用白色畫白線，施寫意技法，畫出工筆效果。

12. 潑墨微韻派－－大氣潑辣的水墨色氣，卻顯出細微神妙的濃郁韻味。

13. 獷細派－－即是粗獷結合細微兩種不同技法，以最粗獷剛硬蒼勁的大寫結合微細工筆於一體，得之出神入化，曠中顯秀。

14. 游絲派－－似如游絲細線勾勒的技法而畫，多於畫人物所用。

15. 版氣派－－即是版畫效果出顯墨氣，感覺上是版畫風格，但內含深藏無窮的自然活潑的氣韻筆觸，是水墨畫並非版畫。

16. 厚堆色塊派－－以堆疊潑辣變化的色塊筆觸，體顯濃厚高度立體韻味，取其抽象和超現實的具象而用色，達到神韻變化莫測、亂而不亂的藝境或寫真效果。

Publisher:
International Art Museum of America
1025 Market St.
San Francisco, CA 94103
Tel# 415-376-6344
www.iamasf.org

ISBN# 978-0-615-50446-9